Easter Island . . . The Pyramids . . . The Piri Reis Map . . . That "Electrified" Ark . . . and a host of other questions . . . The answers are in this book.

"Dr. Wilson is a remarkable man . . . honored as an 'Outstanding Educator of America' in 1971 . . . archaeologist . . . Education professor and Bible scholar."

—Dr. Paul Conrad Berg,
Chair Professor of Education,
University of South Carolina

AN ALTERNATIVE TO

CHARIOTS OF THE GODS?

CLIFFORD WILSON,
M.A., B.D., PH.D.

All quotations from
"Chariots of the Gods?"
are from the second Australian edition.

A LANCER BOOK

CRASH GO THE CHARIOTS

Printed in the U.S.A.

This book has been published by arrangement with
Word of Truth Productions, Ltd., Mt. Waverly, Victoria, Australia.

A TREE HOUSE BOOK

LANCER BOOKS, INC., 1560 BROADWAY
NEW YORK, N.Y. 10036

CRASH GO THE CHARIOTS

By the same author:

IN THE BEGINNING GOD . . .
EXPLORING BIBLE BACKGROUNDS
EXPLORING THE OLD TESTAMENT
NEW LIGHT ON THE GOSPELS
NEW LIGHT ON NEW TESTAMENT LETTERS
ARCHAEOLOGY AND THE BIBLE STUDENT

ASTRONAUT GODS REFUTED

Von Daniken publishes a picture of an old Indian pillar in the center section of his book. The caption tells us that the iron in this pillar does not rust, and that the pillar is hundreds of years old.

The pillar is situated in Delhi and the story of its "special" qualities is well-known . . . However (despite von Daniken's claim to the contrary . . .) it is NOT rust-proof, for it does contain phosphorus and does show signs of some rust though it is remarkably well-preserved. Such a phenomenon does not, however, point to some special technique introduced by astronaut gods, any more than the fact that there were other techniques known to ancient people that would surprise modern scholars.

Contents

FOREWORD

It was no surprise to learn that my friend and colleague at the University of South Carolina, Dr. Clifford Wilson, had written an answer to "Chariots of the Gods?" by Erich von Daniken.

Dr. Wilson is a remarkable man — world traveller, Lecturer of distinction, Archaeologist, Authority in Psycho-linguistics, Education Professor, and Bible Scholar. His unusual gifts were recognized in his being honored as an "Outstanding Educator of America" in 1971 — a fitting distinction for this Australian man of learning.

He has a large listening audience to his "Word of Truth" radio program, and is the producer of a number of audio-visuals relating archaeology to the Bible. He has written several books, and this latest addition will be a valued contribution for a wide reading public who have wondered if there is an answer to Erich von Daniken's hypothesis that astronaut-gods have visited the earth many times during the centuries.

Clifford Wilson's book gives a stimulating answer which deserves serious consideration.

Dr. Paul Conrad Berg,
Chair Professor of Education,
University of South Carolina,
Columbia S.C., U.S.A.
AUGUST 1972

CHAPTER 1

WATCH OUT FOR THOSE ARCHAEOLOGISTS !

In his "Chariots of the Gods?" Erich von Daniken makes statements about archaeologists and archaeology that are quite without foundation — and are often factually in gross error. Just listen to this!

> Scholars make things very easy for themselves. They stick a couple of old potsherds together, search for one or two adjacent cultures, stick a label on the restored find and — hey presto! — once again everything fits splendidly into the approved pattern of thought (at page 37, "Chariots of the Gods?").

Is he serious? At first as I read "Chariots" I could not believe that some of his wild statements were meant to be taken seriously, but, as I read on and came across so many unsupported conjectures, I realized that the man is very much in earnest in his criticisms of many whom I regard as my friends. They are all wrong — according to von Daniken — for in their own interests they "fit into the approved pattern of thought". According to von Daniken this

> is obviously very much simpler than chancing the idea that an embarrassing technical skill might have existed, or the thought of space travellers in the distant past. That would be complicating matters unnecessarily. (page 37)

Such statements are outlandish. Their challenge against scholars who are doing a first-class job in their comparatively new science demands an answer, and it is attempted in these pages. Von Daniken seems to take special delight in attacking archaeologists. He sees a need for panels of experts to replace "archaeologists" as they are thought of today.

My own experience is that archaeological teams are NOT as limited as von Daniken suggests. This was illustrated at Tell Gezer, in Israel, where I was an Area Supervisor. . . .

EXPERTS FROM MANY FIELDS

The team of excavators included world famous names such as Nelson Glueck, G. Ernest Wright, and William Dever. The list of Field and Area Supervisors reads somewhat like a miniature "Who's Who" in archaeology. Names could be listed from disciplines seemingly as wide apart as Geology, History and Theology as well as Archaeology.

Their backgrounds were often radically different, and they came from differing religious persuasions. There were Protestants, Roman Catholics, Jews and agnostics. Some had a special respect for the Bible while others rejected the spiritual tone it demanded.

It was fascinating to listen to men who differed so radically in many ways as they discussed the finds of that particular day — analysing, reconstructing, suggesting, opposing a viewpoint, and agreeing to a new approach where the new facts demanded it.

One point that we should especially stress is that the experts were there — making chemical tests, sifting (literally and figuratively) the evidence, poring over many cross-referencing texts, comparing pottery and other finds with similar artefacts from sites near and far, meticulously recording every aspect of the excavation, with two professional photographers making sure that nothing was missed. There were portable steps to give height, and even a collapsible tower which was moved from area to area as required. Not content with that, Bill Dever — Dr William Dever, Professor of Archaeology at the Hebrew Union College in Jerusalem — utilized a helicopter from time to time to ensure that comprehensive aerial photographs of the best quality were taken.

ARCHAEOLOGISTS FACE THE FACTS

And there were other experts. Darrell Lance (a Professor at Rochester, New York) had all the recorded history of Gezer at his finger-tips; and a number of others had their Ph.D's as specialists in various archaeological time periods, from the bronze age to relatively modern times.

Nor were they inflexible or unwilling to adjust to new facts. I listened to — and even participated in — discussions as to whether a building should be dated to Solomonic or Maccabean times, or whether a cache of Philistine pots could be fitted into accepted chronological dating for pottery remains.

The point of all this is that archaeology is not a discipline consisting only of experts in one particular academic area. Experts in different ancient languages, pottery conservationists, a doctor, theologians of world standing — as well as other experts already mentioned — were at Gezer, reporting for duty at sunrise, and often finishing off their reports about midnight.

They came from many parts of the world — including our Irish architect-surveyor. Some of the Americans found him even harder to understand than me, with my Australian accent! But there was some compensation on that point, for Nelson Glueck told me he liked to talk to me, just to hear my accent. It reminded him of the late Alan Rowe, with whom he had excavated at Beth Shan many years before.

These men were experts in various fields, ready to listen and to adapt. They were true scholars, and would look the evidence squarely in the face even when it seemed that it proved them wrong.

Possibly one of the best examples of that was the late Professor William Foxwell Albright, probably the greatest archaeologist and expert in ancient languages that the world has ever seen, or ever will see. He was not at the excavation of Gezer, but soon afterwards I had a long conversation with him — stretching over several hours, at his home in Baltimore. Part of the time we spent at the nearby Johns Hopkins University where we had lunch and entered into conversation with some of those who now sat where he had sat (he was Professor Emeritus). In much of that discussion I felt like a small boy in the presence of a mental giant, for Dr Albright moved from Accadian to Egyptian hieroglyphics, and to various other ancient languages as he entered with gusto into the topic under discussion.

But it was by no means one-sided. He listened to the opinions of others, ready to concede points as the evidence demanded. It was stimulating to see, and to be the guest of such a man. In a further private conversation afterwards we discussed many of the controversial points of archaeology, and it was again refreshing to realize that this great man had been prepared to change his mind time and time again over the years as he accepted that his earlier tentatively held hypotheses had not always stood the test of fuller investigation.

In passing, it is worth recording that this was especially true as regards *Biblical* archaeology.

Albright made no secret — as his many later writings testify — that his earlier cautious approach to the historical accuracy of the Bible writings had changed drastically. He told me of his personal faith, and of his belief in the Bible as the revelation of God. To some extent his faith was the result of his conviction that the Old Testament writings were remarkably acceptable as genuine historical documents.

But away from the personal. It has been said that Albright shows two faces in his writings — one reading the first edition of "From the Stone Age to Christianity" would hardly recognize that this was the same author who just a few years later presented "The Biblical Period — From Abraham to Ezra." The first showed only limited respect for the authenticity of the sacred historical record, while the latter pointed to the need for a return to a position closely resembling the orthodoxy of a previous day.

Once again, the wheel had turned. But the point we are making is that here is yet another archaeologist (the greatest) freely changing course when the facts demanded it. And the argument could be greatly extended — as to the date of the excavated buildings at Jericho, and of the stables at Megiddo, the nature of the buildings first thought to be furnaces at Ezion-Geber — and many more.

VON DANIKEN'S OPINION OF ARCHAEOLOGISTS

Against this sort of evidence it is relevant to glance at some of the statements of Erich von Daniken. A typical statement is found in the second sentence of his introduction:

> Because its (the book's) theories and proofs do not fit into the mosaic of traditional archaeology, constructed so laboriously and firmly cemented down, scholars will call it nonsense . . .

In the very next paragraph he goes on:

> Nevertheless one thing is certain. There is something inconsistent about our past, that past which lies thousands and millions of years behind us. The past teemed with unknown gods who visited the primaeval earth in manned space-ships.

We shall see that von Daniken does not substantiate his arguments time and time again, and opinions and conclusions are built very quickly on suppositions for which there is no convincing argument according to the normal demands of evidence. We have suggested that archaeologists are NOT limited to theories that are "laboriously and firmly cemented down", but in fact there are very many cases where they have revised when the evidence has demanded.

Here is the sort of argument that von Daniken uses against archaeologists. He tells of gigantic lines that run parallel to each other in the general area of the ancient city of Nazca in Peru, then comments:

> The archaeologists say that they are Inca roads. A preposterous idea! What use were roads that run parallel to each other to the Incas? That intersect? That are laid out in a plain and come to a sudden end? (p. 31)

So the archaeologists are foolish, and the correct answer — according to the author of "Chariots of the Gods?" in his own words, is as follows:

> Seen from the air, the clear-cut impression that the 37-mile-long plain of Nazca made on *me* (italics his) was that of an airfield. (p. 32)

He goes on to say that to classical archaeology "the theory that aircraft could have existed in antiquity is sheer humbug".

True. And to say the least, the author's theory is pure conjecture. I have seen the end of the ancient Roman road near the New Testament city of Jericho — it ends "nowhere". Or go down to the southern part of the Dead Sea, down past the ancient fortress of Masada of Dead Sea Scroll fame. Alongside the sea itself there is the mountain known by the Arabs as Jebel Usdum, Mount Sodom. We shall see that there is good reason to believe that the cities of Sodom and Gomorrah are buried under the Dead Sea at this point, and one of the pieces of evidence is that a Roman road can be photographed from the air. It ends at the Dead Sea and then comes up from the water at the other side. If we had no knowledge of the destruction of those two cities we would be quite without an explanation as to that Roman road.

The fact is, the author of "Chariots" is denying to these ancient Inca people at Nazca the very intelligence and technical know-how which he is in fact demanding for them. It is long since established that there were indeed technical resources and advanced methodology way ahead of what was expected when archaeology was still young 50 years ago, but the flood of archaeological light since then has caused a complete re-assessment. Sir Leonard Woolley's finds at Ur — with gold and silver ornaments, a gold ceremonial dagger, and even a gold ceremonial helmet — are typical of a number of finds that have indicated that people who lived long before Abraham had highly developed civilizations. That ceremonial gold helmet, belonging to Prince Meskalamdug, was not unlike the space helmets which von Daniken ascribes to ancient astronauts. Because of the similarity, must we presume that Meskalamdug was also an astronaut? The evidence points against it, however!

HELPING THE GODS TO LAND

Those Inca people to whom von Daniken refers had a highly developed civilization, and could certainly have had the system of roads that are suggested by archaeologists as the explanation at this point. This is certainly as acceptable as the seemingly wild explanation by von Daniken that they were built by the local people as guide lines for the gods to land by (p. 32). He links with these landing strips a series of drawings found high up on the walls of mountains in Peru. He tells of a figure nearly 820 ft. high that can be observed from a distance of over 12 miles. According to von Daniken, this and others were "enormous drawings that were undoubtedly meant as signals for a being floating in the air . . . what other purpose could they have served?" (p. 33)

What poor argument! We don't know why they were built, why the pictures were drawn, therefore they were undoubtedly signals for the gods! Von Daniken goes on to discuss it, and somewhat modifies his first forthrightness as he writes:

> Their whole activity would have been senseless if the end-product of their efforts had not been meant as signs to beings approaching them from great heights. The stimulating question still has to be answered: why did they do all this if they could have had no idea that flying beings actually existed? (p. 33)

To which we simply say: What about the rock carvings at Behistun? Those inscriptions are about 400 ft. up the side of a mountain which is 1700 ft. high. Did Darius the Great (522-486 B.C.) have any idea of giving signals to "flying beings"? But in fact the inscriptions from that huge work of art high up in the mountains above the trade route have long ago been translated, and they have no mention of being signs for flying beings. They tell rather of the achievements of Darius the Great in the early years of his reign, especially against a usurper and other rebels.

To suggest, because we do not know the answer, that when there are rock inscriptions the only possibility is that flying beings were expected, is clearly poor reasoning.

WHAT NEED FOR A NEW SITE?

If it was a return visit (as per von Daniken), why did they need a *new* landing ground anyway? Why not come in the same way as on the first visit? And those "astronauts" would not land in aeroplanes, but in space-ships surely? So why such extensive landing strips? The archaeological theories that these strange roads are linked with astronomical and calendrical data make much better sense. In any case, as the "landing strips" at Nazca are soft earth, not rock or modern concrete, the jet-stream of the supposed space-ship would blast them away, leaving no trace. These amazing engineers — amazing by von Daniken's own statements! — would certainly not have made earth landing strips.

In the same context the author suggests concerning a huge carving on the rocks that we play at "It looks like . . ." (p. 33). He reminds me of a time when I stood alongside the famous Dead Sea Caves at Qumran. With some of my archaeologist friends and students we were visiting this important area, and we stood looking at those high mountains with their almost-inaccessible caves in which the manuscripts had been hidden.

"Look at that cathedral," one of the group exclaimed suddenly and sure enough there was — and is — a huge cathedral, as though chiselled out of the living mountain. One of the others ridiculed the idea, but this man — not a trained archaeologist by the way —was emphatic that it was in fact a remarkable piece of ancient sculpture. And probably if you look hard enough you'll find such patterns in many unexpected places.

ALL THAT IS LEFT . . . A VISIT FROM SPACE

So much for "It looks like . . ." if you have a good enough imagination. And von Daniken certainly has. That becomes increasingly clear as you read such comments as these:

> Let us suppose that foreign astronauts visited the territory of the Sumerians thousands of years ago. Let us assume that they laid the foundations of the civilisation and culture of the Sumerians and then returned to their own planet, after giving this stimulus to development. Let us postulate that curiosity drove them back to the scene of their pioneer work every hundred terrestrial years to check the results of their experiment. . . . (p. 41)

> We can imagine that 'gods' appeared who collected the semi-savage peoples in the region of Sumer around them and transmitted some of their knowledge to them. (p. 43) . . . all that is left is the hypothesis of a visit from space! (p. 44)

> Without overstretching my imagination, I get the impression that the great god Mars is depicted in a space- or diving-suit. (p. 48)

> (Re space travellers wiping out human freaks) — Admittedly this speculation is full of holes. I shall be told that proofs are lacking. The future will show how many of these holes can be filled in. This book puts forward a hypothesis made up of many speculations. . . . (p. 72)

And there are many others. Our point is that too much of "Chariots" is speculative, with argument based on opinion rather than fact. The author seems to think that vague generalizations as to visitors from space will answer all problems when in fact at best he confuses the issues. True research demands fact rather than imagination, and though an hypothesis can be put forward with the knowledge that it will be challenged, it is expected that there will be a consistent argument based on careful investigation.

THOSE NAZCA "ROADS" AGAIN

As we conclude this section, let us glance at those Nazca "roads" again.

According to von Daniken these lines were "laid out geometrically" and it is "a preposterous idea" to suggest they are Inca roads (p. 31). But he also writes at length about the marvels of the Middle American culture of the Mayas, in many ways a comparable culture. It is interesting to note some of the comments of well-known archaeologist J. Eric S. Thompson about some Maya roads:

> The building of these roads entailed tremendous labor and not a little engineering knowledge. In swampy sections, the engineers had to be sure that their foundations were deep and secure (there are no detours to avoid swampy sections); the lack of any evidence of subsidence demonstrates that they solved the problem. The tracing of the routes must have presented problems, too. The road from Coba to Yaxuna follows these directions: start to mile 4, 279°; mile 4 to mile 10, 269°; mile 10 to mile 15, 260°; mile 15 to mile 20, 270°; mile 20 to mile 40, 260°; mile 40 to mile 62 (Yaxuna), 264° . . . there are two sections of twenty and twenty-two miles respectively without any change of direction. (The Rise and Fall of Maya Civilization, p. 186.)

He goes on to point out that this was a very difficult task with the forest all around the engineer. Elsewhere (p. 75) he refers to an "elaborate network of roads" connecting these cities, and refers to side roads leading to old ruins (p. 186).

It is also relevant to comment that it takes only a few years for such roads to be completely covered by the thick forest vegetation. Thompson tells how at Tikal it was necessary for archaeologists to re-clear the forest from the ruins in 1881, 1904 and 1910 because each time the "vegetation had engulfed the ruins anew" (p. 7).

Thompson points out that the Mayas were inferior to the Aztecs in road building (p. 185), and it is hard to see why von Daniken should argue against the geometric pattern of certain Inca roads. There is clear geometric pattern shown in the quotation above, and the Incas were even better road makers.

ROADS FOR "NON-PRACTICAL" RELIGIOUS PURPOSES

Besides, Eric Thompson gives another relevant point when he tells us that the roads were not built for practical purposes, for the Mayas had no beasts of burden or wheeled vehicles. Rather it seems that they were for spiritual purposes — "as a setting for great religious processions" (p. 189).

He goes on to say that even the corbeled vault would not be employed for utilitarian purposes, but as an embodiment of sacrificial effort. He tells (p. 185) also of a platform 40 feet long and over 16 feet high that covers the road, just before it reaches the outer suburbs of Coba, and it is probable that processions halted at this point to make sacrifices before continuing on into the city.

Anyone who has lived in the East in modern times, and witnessed the great processions (such as Dasara in Mysore City, India) knows something of the extensive nature of the preparations for such occasions, including construction work by "primitive" methods.

Erich von Daniken's "aircraft parking bays" (!) at Nazca could just as easily be explained by a series of roads and sacrificial areas not unlike those described by J. Eric S. Thompson. This would answer von Daniken's question, "What can have induced the pre-Inca peoples to build the fantastic lines, the landing strips, at Nazca?" — far more acceptably than the answer which is implied in his own question.

CHAPTER 2

EASTER ISLAND, THE PYRAMIDS AND EMBALMING

THE PROBLEM OF EASTER ISLAND

To investigate one "mystery" we need to voyage to Easter Island, about 2,000 miles out from Chile. Here the author of "Chariots" has really let his imagination go in an attempt to bolster his theory of visitors from outer space. He tells us:

> An orally transmitted legend tells us that flying men landed and lit fires in ancient times. The legend is confirmed by sculptures of flying creatures with big staring eyes. (p. 115)

For the sake of the theory, it seems a pity that the legend was only orally transmitted. But it is hardly convincing to say it is "confirmed" by the evidence of the flying creatures to which the author refers!

It is interesting to read in "Chariots" some of the results of Thor Heyerdahl's investigations — the man of "Kon-Tiki" fame. Apparently his investigations were accepted as sufficient authority for "Chariots" at certain points. Yet at other points of great importance Heyerdahl is either ignored or overlooked. Von Daniken tells of Heyerdahl discovering hundreds of unfinished statues and thousands of stone implements, including axes (p. 114). But then the author goes off into his own theory—

> The usual explanation, that the stone giants were moved to their present sites on wooden rollers, is not feasible

> in this case, either. . . . Then who cut the statues out of the rock, who carved them and transported them to their sites? How were they moved across country for miles without rollers? How were they dressed, polished and erected? How were the hats, the stone for which came from a different quarry from that of the statues, put in place? (p. 114).

Where do the two authors disagree? One point is as to the number of people who could have lived on the Island — von Daniken says 2,000 while the "Kon-Tiki" man (Heyerdahl) says about 7,000. According to von Daniken "2,000 men was not nearly enough to carve these colossal figures out of the steel-hard volcanic stone with rudimentary tools, even if they worked day and night" (p. 114). In direct contradiction, Heyerdahl suggests that only a few men would be needed to carve the great figures out of volcanic craters, making use of stone axes harder than the rock they were working on. Great quantities of suitable axes were actually found. Von Daniken himself acknowledges this at page 114, yet makes much of the supposed fact that this "steel-hard volcanic rock had been cut through like butter" and goes on to ask how the rock could be cut, dressed and polished (pp. 114-115). The axes would have been used for flaking the rock, then dressing it. Easter Island itself gives this answer, clear to those with "eyes to see."

And von Daniken sees it as an insuperable problem for the limited population to move the statues from their native rock sites to their new resting places some miles away. Our "Kon-Tiki" man supplied the answer long ago. He estimated that about a thousand men would have been required to pull the statues from the quarry site, but only about 500 would have been needed to transport them to their new "home" where inclined ramps had previously been prepared. The statues were dragged up feet first and toppled over into the prepared hole after which the 'hat' of a different stone was dragged up the ramp and placed in position.

The evidence supports Heyerdahl rather than von Daniken, for — as is acknowledged in "Chariots" — Heyerdahl discovered hundreds of unfinished statues on the island, and some of the old inclined ramps are still standing.

AKU-AKU, THE SECRET OF EASTER ISLAND

The death-knell to von Daniken's hypothesis at this point comes from a later book by Thor Heyerdahl, "Aku-Aku, the Secret of Easter Island" (1958). It makes fascinating reading.

Three stories of particular interest relate to the commencement of the making of a new Easter Island statue; another to the re-erection of one of the fallen colossae; and the third to the actual movement of an Easter Island statue across the plain. They are told in continuous narrative form, and are fascinating reading at pages 132 to 151 of "Aku-Aku." Photographs are supplied in color, forever dispelling much of the mystery surrounding these famous old statues. And those photographs are irrefutable evidence demanding the rejection of von Daniken's hypothesis at this point.

Here is a brief summary of the three stories.

On Easter Island, Thor Heyerdahl was told that the mayor was a member of the only family descended from the "long-ears" (artificially made so) who had been responsible for the original statues. After the right approaches had been made, the mayor was released from his mayoral duties so that he and his relatives (only descendants from the "long-ears" were eligible) could carve a statue. This was begun by six men after indulging in "necessary" religious ceremonials, and they used abandoned stone picks which were in the quarry, "literally in hundreds" (p. 135).

A NEW STATUE TAKES SHAPE

Heyerdahl writes:

> Stroke followed stroke, the rock was hard; stone against stone, the little pick was the harder and the rock must give way. Clink-clink-clink, the blows of the picks must have been heard far out over the plain. For the first time in centuries the clink of stone was heard in Rano Raraku. . . .
>
> Not much of a mark was made by each blow, hardly more than a grey patch of dust, but with another blow, and one more, and still another, something was gained. And at intervals the men grabbed the calabash and splashed water on the rock face, to soften it where they cut . . . (p. 136)

By the third day the contours of the newly created giant were "clearly visible on the rock wall". As a stone axe was blunted the mayor struck it against another on the ground, with splinters flaking off, "and he produced a new point as easily as a clerk sharpens a pencil" (p. 137). Heyerdahl goes on to tell that an average statue of fifteen feet high would require the services of about six men — the unfinished statues had been left because of technical flaws, such as a crack in the rock, and not because of lack of manpower.

The mayor estimated that it would take a year to complete the statue, which was longer than the visitors could allow, but the purpose of the exercise had been accomplished, for "the mayor and his men had now shown us the technique of the sculptors" (p. 137).

HOW WERE THE STATUES RAISED?

The second point of interest was, "How were the statues raised?" and again the mayor had the answer. When asked why he had not told it before, his dignified reply was, "No one asked *me*" (p. 142). On the promise of $100 payment, he agreed to have one of the biggest statues restored to its proper "home" on the temp'e wall. And he with 11 other men did just that . . . as the photographic evidence in "Aku-Aku" establishes. First, three large wooden poles were used to lift the statue just a fraction of an inch, and the mayor forced small stones underneath it. This process was repeated and repeated many times, with the stones getting larger and larger, and the statue was roped into place to prevent it toppling over.

This statue was nearly ten feet wide across the shoulders, and weighed between 25 and 30 tons (p. 145). After one day only two poles were used, with five men on each. The mayor's youngest brother now became the "stone pusher", while the mayor himself became a sort of foreman, and actually beat the air in time as he encouraged them on, in his own language, "One, two, three! One, two, three! Hold on, push under! Once more! One, two, three! One, two, three!" (p. 146). Remarkably like the "heave-ho" method which Erich von Daniken disparages!

The end of the operation is described very dramatically by Thor Heyerdahl. On the eighteenth day the two teams were working cautiously as they worked on their ropes from opposite ends — one group on the beach and the other in the middle of the camp. All of a sudden the giant statue began to move perceptibly, and the order to halt was immediately given. Heyerdahl writes:

> The giant rose in all his might and began to tilt upright, the supporting pole was left standing without a counterpoise, a rumbling and sliding of

> stone began, and great blocks came crashing down on top of one another in a cloud of smoke and dust. But the colossus only wobbled and came quietly to rest in an upright position (p. 148).
>
> The mystery of how the statues were raised had been resolved, and the stone "hat" on the statue could be raised in exactly the same way. The tower of stones could be taken away when both statue and cap were in position (p. 151).

MOVING THE STATUES ACROSS THE PLAIN

Heyerdahl's third point was that the stone statues could be moved across the countryside of Easter Island. He arranged a great feast which was thoroughly enjoyed by the villagers. Then in something of a game 180 men took their places on a long rope that had been attached to one statue's neck. At the first effort the rope broke, and the mayor was a little embarrassed, but he ordered the rope to be doubled and made fast again.

> Now the giant began to move — first in short jerks, but then suddenly it seemed to break loose . . . the long lines of natives hauled patiently and yelled at the tops of their voices with enthusiasm. It moved as quickly as if they each were hauling an empty soap box (p. 150).

The statue that the mayor and his men raised has once again become "a landmark visible far out to sea" (opp. p. 193). It is a silent but convincing answer to Erich von Daniken's hypothesis that "the 'heave-ho' method . . . would have been impossible on Easter Island for lack of manpower" (p. 114 "Chariots").

And so another von Daniken "Chariot" has crashed, brought down in flames by one of the very witnesses that seemed so impressively to bolster his way-out theories.

"WHAT TITANIC FORCE TURNED IT UPSIDE DOWN?"

Before we leave the general area of South America let us comment briefly on another matter — that huge block pictured by von Daniken, at Sacsayhuaman in Peru. He asks, "What titanic force turned it upside down?" The answer is simple — an earthquake. The area is in the great earthquake chain of South America. Do we need "titanic forces" to explain earthquake damage today? Surely not "titanic forces" of the von Daniken type!

Even if this were not in an earthquake region (as it is), von Daniken's space-gods would not be needed to turn a huge block over. J. Eric S. Thompson in "The Rise and Fall of Maya Civilization" has an interesting comment, indirectly relevant. It seems that after the overthrow of the rulers at Tikal in Guatemala, the masons were won over to the rebels and they attempted a measure of restoration and—

> At Tikal broken stelae were reset, even upside down (p. 106).

Although not as huge as von Daniken claims for the megalith in Peru, a number of huge stones are incorporated in ancient constructions such as the Mortuary Temple of Mycerinus and the Temple of Solomon. Most of the massive stones in other buildings were much smaller than the largest of these, but these occasional megaliths make it clear that not only were huge slabs lifted and transported, but they were also placed in their appointed positions . . . without astronauts!

WHAT ABOUT THOSE PYRAMIDS?

It is a natural "jump" from huge stones and buildings to the Pyramids, so we shall visit Egypt.

Excavations were proceeding at Karnak, famous for so much recovered life from Egypt's past.

I introduced myself to the French leader of the current excavations, but did not detain him, for it was obvious that he had much more to occupy his mind than a visitor from "down under". So I quietly wandered around, watching as huge stones, weighing about a ton each, were hauled back into the positions they had occupied long centuries before, back in those days when the Pharaoh's word was law in Egypt.

One group especially fascinated me — about 10 men, with a foreman supervising, using primitive pulley methods to lift those great stones. It was all done to music — perfect timing, with the actual new thrust taking place at just the right moment of the chant they were all singing.

This is along the lines of the "heave-ho" method to which von Daniken refers as the method suggested by "people with lively imaginations" (p. 114). I was watching a modern enactment of a scene that must have taken place for long periods as the Pyramids were constructed.

In this same context von Daniken writes caustically as to the possibility that these "12-ton blocks were pushed skyward" by this "heave-ho" method. (p. 101). It is more usual to estimate the weight at about 2½ tons each — about one-fifth the size von Daniken puts forward. However, many were very much larger.

But let us go back down the Nile, away from fantastic Karnak, Thebes, and the nearby Valley of the Kings. Down to Gizeh, just a few miles outside Cairo, to those mighty Pyramids. Actually there are many of them, stretching in a great line along the Nile, but the most famous are at Gizeh, and von Daniken refers to these.

According to the author of "Chariots" one of the great problems was wood — which the Egyptians could not have imported in sufficient quantity because they did not have a large enough fleet (p. 97). Nor would they have made wooden rollers from their native trees, for the dates from the palms were urgently needed for food, and the trunks and fronds provided shelter for the dried-up land — so states von Daniken.

However, wood WAS used extensively for other purposes in ancient Egypt, as a visit to the Cairo Museum will soon demonstrate. Tutankhamen's treasures are but one indication of the large amount of wood that was used for furniture and other purposes. Wooden sledges were utilized in the construction of the pyramids, and so was wooden scaffolding. Wood was used extensively—I. E. S. Edwards tells of wooden baulks found *in situ* at Lisht. The fact is, while all the details of construction are not yet known, enough evidence is available from Egyptian reliefs to give the general picture. Rafts were used to float the limestone and granite blocks to within a few hundred yards of the Pyramids when the Nile was in flood. This was an annual event, though there were many times when poverty was rife because the Nile did NOT overflow.

HOW LONG TO BUILD A PYRAMID?

Von Daniken's greatest criticism of traditionally held beliefs about the Pyramids relates to the time it would take to build them. He argues that several hundred thousand workmen would be required, and if they worked extraordinarily fast they could have completed the Great Pyramid of the Pharaoh Khufu in 664 years (p. 101). The author of "Chariots" then implies that this is totally unacceptable, and says:

> It seems obvious to me that the Pyramid cannot have been erected during a single lifetime.

This being the case, according to von Daniken, the Pharaoh Khufu conceivably forged the inscriptions that proclaimed his fame, and the Pyramid would have been erected "long before Khufu left his visiting card".

Who then really built the Great Pyramid? Von Daniken gives a "possible" answer — the Egyptian King Surid who ruled in Egypt before the Flood (p. 102). Presumably this solves the problem of the hundreds of years required for the construction, for von Daniken has already referred to the Kings "before the Flood" who lived — according to the Sumerian King List — for hundreds of years. If this is how he solves the problem, it follows that he is accepting literally that these kings lived for so long — for on the one hand he requires over 600 years for the erection of the Pyramid; and argues that this is not possible in the life of one king. As he accepts that King Surid had the Pyramid built (p. 102), it follows that King Surid must have lived, according to von Daniken, for over 600 years.

But von Daniken says that the Sumerian figures are "physically impossible" (p. 106). Presumably we must therefore not allow for the possibility of an Egyptian Pharaoh living for this great period of time that von Daniken needs for the building of the Pyramids.

In his "Critical Review" of "Chariots of the Gods?" my successor as Director of the Australian Institute of Archaeology, Mr. Gordon Garner, provides valuable information at this point. Ahmed Fakhry ("The Pyramids") and I. E. S. Edwards ("The Pyramids of Egypt") are likewise relevant. Each shows a picture from the tomb of Djehutihotep, a 12th Dynasty nobleman. Edwards says:

> In this scene an alabaster statue of Djehutihotep, which probably weighed about 60 tons, is mounted

on a sledge pulled by 172 men. Water or some other liquid is poured on the ground to lessen the friction and thus facilitate haulage (p. 266).

This colossus was over 6.5 meters high, and was on a wooden sledge that was dragged along by ropes.

PHARAOHS' NAMES ON PYRAMIDS

The names of some of the Pharaohs are inscribed on blocks in various Pyramids. (Edwards pp. 110ff, 205, 223, 238.)

These facts of history are not as mysterious as von Daniken implies.

We have already stated that the Great Pyramid is only one of many stretching along the Nile, and one of these is the Pyramid of Meidum. Blocks have been located in this Pyramid with different dates at various points. Another Pyramid at Dahshur actually has a date on the north-eastern corner stone — it was laid in the 21st year of Pharaoh Senefru. About half-way up there is another date, this time dating to the same Pharaoh's 22nd year. If the dating is accurate, the maximum between the two would be under two years. This Pyramid is about two-thirds the volume of the Great Pyramid, and even if the dates given are not accurate — perhaps the boastful exaggeration of the Pharaoh's builders — it is clear that nothing like the 664 years demanded by von Daniken is required.

The ancient historian Herodotus says it took 20 years and four separate groups of 100,000 men (each group working for three months of the year) to build the actual Pyramid. An extra 10 years was said to be taken for building the causeway across which the stone had to be hauled after being transported from its landing point at the nearby Nile. The work on the substructures went on at the same time.

Even this figure of 20 years for the actual Pyramid seems longer than the case demands — and Cheops, for whom the Great Pyramid was built, reigned only about 22 years (Edwards, p. 168; see also p. 283).

My mind goes again to those huge blocks recovered and being restored at Karnak, and to the remarkable achievements of a comparatively small group of modern Egyptian workmen.

Did it take 600 years to build the Pyramid? No! Surely another "Chariot" has crashed, this time into the base of the Great Pyramid of the Pharoah Khufu (or Cheops, the Greek form of his name).

CALCULATIONS FROM THE GREAT PYRAMID

We quote from von Daniken:

> Is it really a coincidence that the height of the Pyramid of Cheops multiplied by 1,000 million corresponds approximately to the distance between the earth and sun? That is to say, 93 million miles. (p. 99)

The calculation is easily made. The height of the Pyramid is 481.4 feet and there are 5,280 feet to a mile. Therefore the distance would be 91.17 million miles. If we are to accept von Daniken's statements about the fantastic accuracy of these ancient records we would expect a much closer degree of accuracy than that. In any case, why should we multiply the height of the Pyramid by 1,000 million — just to build up a theory we have already decided on?

His calculation for "pi" is open to similar challenge and rejection. The sides of the square base of the Pyramid of Cheops are approximately 756 feet long, and the equation given by von Daniken would work out as follows: 756 x 756 = 571,536, and divided by 962 this gives 594.1, very different from pi which is 3.1416!

Before we leave Egypt, let us consider another peculiar hypothesis, this time about embalming.

STRANGE TALK ABOUT EMBALMING

It had been an interesting conversation, especially as my host, the Director of the Cairo Museum, spoke English fluently. Our conversation ranged over many aspects of archaeology, not the least important being the near-embarrassment Egypt suffers at having such huge quantities of recovered artefacts from ancient Egyptian sites. This is obvious to even the casual visitor — for he sees a huge statue of Rameses II in the mud alongside the formerly sacred pool (now a stagnant water-hole) at Memphis, and even those magnificent Colossae of Memnon stand in a farmer's field, unattended except by his silent crops.

I assured the Director I did not want a personally conducted tour of the Museum, for there was so much I wanted to see and to photograph for myself: the Stela of Pharaoh Merneptah, with its first historic reference to Israel as a nation; the famous Tutankhamen tomb findings; the mummies of Egyptian Pharaohs, and many more recovered treasures. So I was given a free pass, and had a most enjoyable morning wandering around, photographing, questioning, making notes — and not the least of my enjoyments was my time in the "mummy room". And that brings me to the point of this story.

I presented my pass at the door, only to be told that I still must pay. I insisted that I had a free pass — there it was, in perfectly good Egyptian script. But the attendant was determined — I must pay. So I asked him to bring me to the Supervisor, for it had become — I confess! — something of a personality clash (though I made sure that was happily resolved later).

"You must pay to get into the mummy room," stated the Supervisor.

"No," I said, equally determined by now, "Here is my ticket — signed by your Director. I am to have free admission to the Museum."

The Supervisor looked at the ticket again, then his eyes lit up.

"You must pay," he said, slamming the ticket down in triumph. "This is only for admission to the Museum, and there is a special charge for admission to the mummy room." I saw the funny side of the incident, and with a grin paid up the nominal extra charge.

WIZENED OLD PHARAOHS

In a way, the mummy room was somewhat of a disappointment. I looked at the famous Seti I — one of Egypt's crueller rulers, though a renowned military campaigner. There in a glass case was his actual head — like a wizened old, old man, his jugular vein protruding in a most gruesome way. And this seemed to be the picture right around the room. It was enough to scare you off mummies for the rest of your life. Though I suppose life would be rather odd with only daddies.

All this is somewhat of an introduction to the subject of embalming that Erich von Daniken raises. He asks:

> Or did some gods (= space travellers) transmit their knowledge of how corpses can be reawakened after a special treatment to a quick-witted prince of royal blood? . . . .
>
> The high priests, who actually did possess some knowledge of such reawakenings, did a great deal to encourage this cult, for their class did good business out of it. . . . Are we perhaps getting a clue to the incredible age of the men named in the texts if we assume that they were mummified or frozen? (pp. 106-7)

Much more follows, and it becomes clear that the author of "Chariots" is putting forward the theory that mummification is in the same category as modern ideas of deep-freezing bodies for "reawakening" hundreds or thousands of years later when medical techniques have been perfected. He talks about frozen blood, preserved human bones, deep-freeze cemeteries — and embalming.

But this association is quite unjustified by the facts. While not advocating that there is such a possibility of frozen bodies being thawed out when medical advance ensures greater longevity of life, it should be recognized that those new ideas are quite different from the processes involved in the Egyptian practice of embalming.

The four sons of the god Horus were supposed to sit on the tops of four funerary jars, and in those jars were placed various internal organs of the deceased person. Even the heart was removed — I have seen inscriptions in the Valley of the Kings showing a man's heart being weighed against the feather of truth.

Despite the argument of Erich von Daniken as to embalming and reawakenings in this life, this was NOT the Egyptian hope. Rather they were to pronounce certain magic formulae in the life beyond the grave, so that their inward parts would return to their bodies and a new life would commence. They thought of this as having some continuum with the present life, for man conceives of himself as eternal when blessed of the gods; and man's body is part of himself. In some way the Egyptians could not understand or explain, the body would be involved in that future life. And so token amounts of food were placed in the tombs, together with wooden ushabti (servants), and various other implements that spoke of the continuation of life. But even a Pharaoh could not provide enough food for an eternal lifetime. Relatively, the amounts in the tombs were of a token form.

Strangely, the Egyptians do not seem to have preserved the brain, this also being removed before embalming took place. What sort of a future earthly life could be promised to a man who was revived without a brain? The possibility is of course absurd — despite von Daniken's hypothesis.

The dry desert climate sometimes made possible the preservation of a body without embalming, and this probably is the natural explanation behind the Egyptian practice.

But at one point von Daniken is right — the Egyptians DID have some idea of immortality, and perhaps there is an answer to his question as to where this idea first came from (p. 105).

MAN IS DISTINCTIVE IN THREE WAYS

The archaeological evidence indicates that man is distinct from all other creatures in three separate ways. He has an inherent knowledge that there is a power beyond himself: so, in site after site, images of gods and altars are found. But no bird, no animal, ever made such an image or built an altar to a god. This fits the Bible statement that man is made in the image of God — of God Who is infinite, God Who is eternal. Man has a strange understanding of his own potential, his own share in the nature of that eternal God. He seeks for that God or gods, and believes that he himself will somehow live for ever in the presence of God or gods.

A knowledge of God, a belief in life beyond the grave, and the ability to communicate by spoken words — these are distinctively human, and this is borne out by archaeological research.

And the ancient Egyptians who practised embalming and left food and implements in their graves were simply demonstrating that they, too, had joined a long line of peoples across the face of the globe who had in many ways shown that they have such beliefs.

CHAPTER 3

THAT SURPRISING CLAIM ABOUT THE ELECTRIFIED ARK

Von Daniken collates many facts from many areas, areas of learning as well as geographic areas. But at times his writing is ludicrous — with pathetically weak statements that surely cannot be taken seriously. One of the weakest examples is what he has to say about the Ark of the Covenant. This was a chest in which Moses was to place certain sacred objects, all with spiritual significance, and precise instructions were given as to the size and covering of this very special box. When the Israelites were on the march it was to be carried only by divinely appointed persons, and it was to be treated as a holy object, for it spoke by symbols of the Being of God. The Christian sees very clear spiritual significance in all this, for the objects placed inside that box were of spiritual and historical significance — the tablets of the law, a pot of the manna from the wilderness, and Aaron's rod which especially spoke of newness of life with God.

An incident is recorded at II Samuel chapter 6 of a man named Uzzah grabbing the Ark and being struck dead, at the time when King David was moving it towards Jerusalem. Uzzah had paid the price for sacrilege.

"UNDOUBTEDLY THE ARK WAS ELECTRICALLY CHARGED!"

Von Daniken apparently does not doubt the fact of the incident, but this is how he explains it:

> When passing cattle shook and threatened to overturn the Ark, Uzzah grabbed hold of it. He fell dead on the spot, as if struck by lightning. Undoubtedly the Ark was electrically charged! (p. 59)

Unfortunately this is typical of the approach in "Chariots". A fact of history is taken, it is recognized that there is an apparent difficulty in explaining it, so a way-out theory is put forward as the one possible solution. So, in this case, the sacred Ark of the Covenant was electrically charged! Nonsense.

I'm no electrical expert, so I called my friend Geoff Peers — an electronics technician. He took time to check his facts, then called me back. What Geoff had to say confirmed my own thinking.

The conversation went something like this:—

WILSON: Geoff, what about von Daniken's claim that the Ark of the Covenant must have been electrically charged when Uzzah was struck dead for touching it?

PEERS: Yes, I've already gone into that — I'll check out a few things and call you back.
(Which he did.)

WILSON: Don't be too technical Geoff — would it be possible for the Ark to have been electrically charged?

PEERS: I've now discussed this theory with the instructors at the college where I myself was trained. There are a number of things that ought to be said.

WILSON: Right. Let's start with von Daniken's claim that a condenser was formed by the gold plates, one being positive and the other negative.

PEERS: If we take a cubit as being 18 inches, the Ark was a box about 3' 9" x 2' 3" x 2' 3". The instructions given to Moses are very clear — the wood of the box was to be completely overlaid with gold. The rings on the corners were also to be overlaid with gold, and so were the staves with which the Ark was to be carried.

WILSON: Are you saying that there was virtually only ONE metal plate, and so there was no possibility of there being one negative and one positive?

PEERS: Yes — if it was charged any one part would be in fact part of the rest, and the conditions needed for a condenser are simply not fulfilled. There would automatically be a short circuit.

WILSON: What are the requirements for a condenser?

PEERS: There must be two pieces that are separated by an insulator. Theoretically it is possible for there to be only one piece of metal, but it would need to have an insulator — for example, a piece of wood — in the middle so that for the purposes of the condenser the metal was acted upon as though it was two pieces of metal, separated by the wood. The technical name for the insulating piece of wood is the dielectric.

WILSON: And all this was not possible with the Ark because it was completely overlaid with gold —there was no insulator to make possible a negative and a positive plate?

PEERS: That's right. And what's more, over the top of the Ark the Mercy Seat was placed, and it was made of pure gold. It was exactly the same length and breadth as the Ark, and so it fitted completely over the top. Even if von Daniken argued that somehow there was a space inside (which is not so according to the Bible), that space would have been completely covered by the Mercy Seat on the top.

WILSON: So no one could put his hand inside to make contact with the supposed two plates?

PEERS: Exactly — so even if we accepted von Daniken's hypothesis even though it opposes the instructions given to Moses, there would still not be a condenser.

WILSON: So when Uzzah touched the Ark he was not killed by an electric charge given out from a condenser?

PEERS: That's not all. A condenser must be charged, and it is a perfectly legitimate question to ask, "Where did the electricity come from to charge a condenser?" For the condenser is simply a storage place of electricity. Where did Moses plug in for power in the first place?

STATIC ELECTRICITY?

WILSON: Excuse the silly question — but what about static electricity? Sometimes you can get a small charge when you get out of a motor car, when you move from the insulation of the rubber tyres and so on.

PEERS: It's not a silly question, but it still could not explain Uzzah's death. The comparable situation to the motor car would be for the whole ark to become one "plate" and for the earth itself to become the other — the insulator between them would be the air gap. But the greater the air gap the smaller the electric charge, and even in a motor car you don't get anything like a fatal shock — usually only a few volts. To get a fatal shock you need enough volts and enough amperage as well. When you touch the spark on a motor engine you can be in contact with as much as 15,000 volts, but it is not fatal because the amperage is not there. On the other hand you can still not be killed when you put your fingers across the terminal of a car battery, for though there might be 100 amps there is only 12 volts — you must have both the amperage and the volts for the shock to be so effective as to kill a man.

WILSON: In any case, if it killed Uzzah surely it would also kill the priests?

PEERS: That's another point. I've made a careful search of the Bible references and there is nothing said about the priests having protective clothes or special shoes. If a man such as Uzzah, in contact with the supposed "earth plate", could be killed by "joining" the plates — that is, the earth and the Ark, it stands to reason that the priests also would be killed every time they touched the ground or touched anyone or anything in contact with the ground. They carried the Ark at times, as when they placed it in this cart, and then in a man's house.

WILSON: So if von Daniken's hypothesis was correct, the priests also must have been killed?

PEERS: That's right. Even their carrying poles were completely covered with gold, so they were automatically in contact with what von Daniken is referring to as the metal plates.

WILSON: Von Daniken is of course making a case that Moses was given very specific instructions because of the special nature of this object as a means of communication. Any comment?

PEERS: I've been studying that too. The fact is that God gave very specific instructions for ALL that was associated with the Tabernacle which was to symbolise His presence in the midst of His people. Everyday things like dishes and spoons were included — but von Daniken makes nothing of that at all. He has missed the whole point of the instructions, for as these things were set apart they were reminding the Israelites that spiritual values touched all departments of life.

This was not just a magical formula, or a new revelation of science as to electric power.

WILSON: So you don't think Uzzah died of an electric shock?

PEERS: There is no mention of it in the Bible — von Daniken says he died "as if struck by lightning. Undoubtedly the Ark was electrically charged!" There simply is no basis for this claim: it is nothing but an unwarranted assumption. In fact, if we go over to Numbers chapter 4 verse 15 we find that the warning is given that if someone touched ANY of the holy things, that person would die. The same sort of warning was given when Moses was receiving the Law on Mount Sinai — the Israelites dared not approach the mountain.

THE CHERUBIM AS A MICROPHONE

WILSON: You've done your homework well! Let's move on to von Daniken's claim that one of the cherubim figures above the Ark could have been used as a microphone. Any comment?

PEERS: The Bible makes it clear that this simply was not the case. At Exodus 25:22 it states that God would commune with Moses from BETWEEN the cherubim ABOVE the Mercy Seat. Von Daniken states that God would "speak to him from the mercy seat" and then suggests that "one of the two cherubim on the mercy seat acted as a magnet, the loudspeaker . . ." Both statements are at page 58 of his book. The verse I've just quoted makes it clear that von Daniken is wrong in both his assumptions, provided we take the Bible literally, as von Daniken himself is doing at this point.

WILSON: What about this whole idea of a magnet and a loudspeaker — would it technically be possible in association with the Ark?

PEERS: This would have to be a condenser microphone of course. In such a microphone the two plates would move in and out from the dielectric — that's the insulating strip between the two plates. It's only a fractional movement, and the voltage varies according to the distance moved — the further the plates are apart, the lower the voltage. A microphone works on vibrations moving the parts that make it up, thus producing varying charges of electricity — as when the diaphragm of a telephone pulls up and down as a conversation proceeds. This causes an electric current which is then amplified — and so on.

WILSON: Are you saying the cherubim COULD have been used as von Daniken suggests?

PEERS: No. Technically the Ark as described in the Bible could not be made in such a way that it would act as a microphone or speaker, and in any case it would not be possible physically even if the instructions to Moses were changed and a condenser was made. The amount of voltage produced by such a condenser would register at something like 10 to the minus 6 — only millionths part of one volt. It would be quite impossible to use it to send out the volume of noise required to communicate with a space ship, as von Daniken suggests at page 58. The whole thing is ludicrous.

WILSON: Could we use it as von Daniken suggests now that we have our modern scientific knowledge?

PEERS: No. The voltage level would be much too low, and you need other electronic gear besides a condenser to make contact. Even the essential coils of wire are not referred to in the precise instructions given to Moses. This particular aspect was not discovered until 1819 by a man named Ersted — over 3000 years after the time of Moses. He showed the relationship between magnetism and electricity.

WILSON: You mentioned "magnetism" — von Daniken refers to a magnet in this context. Any comment?

PEERS: The use of the magnet was not known until the times of the Greeks, many hundreds of years after Moses. They called it a lode stone. In the days of Moses there was no knowledge of the fact that vibrations could cause electricity, let alone being able to implement all the complexities involved in verbal communication with a space ship.

Our conversation continued for some time, as my friend explained technical points. If I had not been convinced before, I certainly was now. Von Daniken's hypothesis simply does not stand serious investigation.

"WITHOUT ACTUALLY CONSULTING EXODUS . . ."

But this "electrically charged" criticism does not end there. In the same paragraph in which he says, "Undoubtedly the Ark was electrically charged!" von Daniken also says:

> Without actually consulting Exodus, I seem to remember that the Ark was often surrounded by flashing sparks and that Moses made use of this "transmitter" whenever he needed help and advice. (pp. 58-59)

Is this meant to be taken as evidence of serious research? In his own words we find that he puts forward part of his way-out theory "without actually consulting Exodus". There are far too many Bible critics who know all about the Bible, tell you it's full of mistakes and so on, but cannot put their finger on one when they are handed a Bible. Von Daniken makes his case even weaker when he goes on to say, "I seem to remember." Fancy relying on such a vague approach when he is presenting a view which will be disturbing to thousands of Christians, and Jews too, as they read!

"I seem to remember." "Without actually consulting Exodus." The pity is that he did NOT consult Exodus, for in fact his memory has let him down. There is no reference in Exodus — or anywhere else in Scripture — of the Ark being "surrounded by flashing sparks".

And that is not all. There are a number of occasions recorded in this very Book of Exodus where God speaks to Moses BEFORE the Ark was constructed. Exodus chapter 6 records one of a number of such occasions. What was the "transmitter" used on those occasions? The Bible certainly does not support the ideas of Erich von Daniken at this point.

Sadly, the "Chariots of the Gods" have been short-circuited again. . . . They crash in searing flames when confronted by the evidence from an old Book which a Psalmist once referred to as a light — "A light unto my path." And a New Testament writer commented that that same "Word of God" is full of power — "The Word of God is quick, and powerful" (Hebrews 4:12). It has been called "That Impregnable Rock of Holy Scripture." Through the centuries it has been well able to defend itself. It will continue to do so despite the wild theories of Erich von Daniken and the question he asks on the cover of his book, "Was God an Astronaut?"

CHAPTER 4

OUTFLOODING THE FLOOD

Erich von Daniken has many strange views, as revealed in "Chariots". Yet another relates to the story of the great Flood which is recorded in the Bible. Some scholars raise such questions as whether it was "local" (confined to the Fertile Crescent) or "universal" (world-wide), but Erich von Daniken "outfloods" them all. He has the original version coming from South America! This is his viewpoint relating to the famous "Epic of Gilgamesh".

First we shall consider the main facts of the Epic itself, and make some comments as to the Biblical record.

Archaeologically the author is simply way off the facts. Perhaps it should first be stated that this Epic is the Babylonian record of the Flood, a record that was copied by the Assyrians at a much later time.

"PARALLEL TO GENESIS"

Von Daniken makes the claim that "the main thread of the Epic of Gilgamesh runs parallel to the Biblical Book of Genesis" (p. 64), but in fact the similarity of this Epic to the Bible record is limited to the Flood story. The Babylonian Creation story is known as Enuma Elish (from the first words, meaning "When from above . . .") while a more recently translated Epic — the Epic of Atrahasis — brings together parts of the other two Epics. But none of them pre-date the Biblical record which is now recognized as the oldest of all these records, and certainly it is not copied from the Babylonian version. Von Daniken has the Bible account as a second-hand one (p. 68), but the evidence is against such an argument. As Professor W. F. Albright points out in his "Yahweh and the Gods of Canaan", the Bible record contains archaic features dating it before any Mesopotamian version that is "preserved in cuneiform sources" (in "Yahweh and the gods of Canaan," Athlone Press, London, 1968, p. 86). Those cuneiform sources include the Epic of Gilgamesh and the Epic of Atrahasis.

The Bible account is not the second-hand one. Rather the Babylonian and Assyrian versions are later distortions, with many differences from the Bible record. The superiority of the Bible version is established.

To substantiate such a statement, let us look at the facts. First, we need briefly to summarise the Epic of Gilgamesh as it relates to the Flood.

WHAT THE EPIC IS ALL ABOUT

Utnapishtim was the Babylonian Noah, and with his boatman Puzu-Amurri he went through seven days of terrible flood. A very good friend of Gilgamesh named Enkidu had died at the decree of the gods, and Gilgamesh realised that he too must eventually die. He heard of Utnapishtim, who had escaped death, and he set out to find him so that he could learn from him the secret of immortality. Gilgamesh eventually found Utnapishtim, the only man who had ever obtained everlasting life. Gilgamesh asked Utnapishtim how he found this secret. Utnapishtim then told how one of the gods urged him to destroy his house and build a vessel. Utnapishtim obeyed the voice of the gods, built a great boat, and eventually the expected flood came.

GODS COWERING LIKE DOGS

Before long the gods themselves were terrified, and we read:

> "Even the gods were afeared at the deluge, took to flight and went up to the heaven of Anu, cowered they like dogs and crouched down at the outer defences."

That certainly is a very different concept of God from that given in the Bible record of the flood. We surely could not think of the God of the Bible cowering like a dog or being terrified by a deluge.

Another translation of the Epic tells of the goddess Ishtar in great distress:

"Ishtar cried like a woman in travail, wailed the queen of the gods with her beautiful voice: 'Those creatures are turned to clay, since I commanded evil in the assembly of the gods; because I commanded evil in the assembly of the gods, for the destruction of my people I commanded battle. I alone bore my people; like spawn of fishes they fill the sea.' The gods along with the Anunnaki wept with her, the gods bowed, sat as they wept; closed were their lips; (silent their) assembly."

The crude polytheism of this Babylonian Epic is obviously vastly different from the majestic, yet simple, Bible record.

When the flood was all over and Utnapishtim came out, he made an offering to the gods, and the Epic of Gilgamesh tells us:

> "And the gods smelled the savour, the gods smelled the sweet savour, the gods gathered like flies about the priest of the offering."

These poor gods had not been fed — because mankind had been destroyed, and so they gathered like flies as soon as Utnapishtim remembered their need and did something about it! The God Who is revealed in the Bible does not need the offerings of a man to sate His hunger, nor could we ever imagine it being said of the true God of the Heavens that He has come like flies to an offering.

After that the gods were angry amongst themselves, and began to blame each other for their foolishness in bringing this flood on man. It is all very different from the Bible picture of God waiting patiently while a Gospel of mercy was preached. The true God acted in judgment only when man continued to reject His ways.

SIMILARITIES — AND DIFFERENCES

Other writers besides von Daniken have pointed to similarities to the Bible story: thus in each record there is supposedly a final revelation to the hero of the flood, warning him that a deluge is coming which is unknown to everyone else. However, in the Bible story, Noah is told to warn others so that they too can accept the way of salvation if they so desire.

In each case the hero builds a vessel which is pitched within and without with pitch, describes the flood in which all others are destroyed, tells of the great ship resting on a mountain, and of certain birds being sent out. Each record tells how the hero disembarks and offers a sacrifice, and it then says that such a deluge shall not be visited on man again.

However, the dissimilarities are even more important than the similarities, and they clearly point to the fact that the Babylonian version is a corruption of the Biblical original.

The Bible account is, as we have seen, very different from the Babylonian legend. The gross polytheism of the Babylonian story, with gods crouching with fear, and then swarming like hungry flies to a sacrifice, is quite alien to the noble concept of the almighty God presented in the Bible record.

Thus, as we compare the Babylonian and other ancient records of the Flood with the Bible record, it becomes clear that the Bible record is infinitely superior. It does not bear the marks of the grotesque, the superstitious or the magical. Its description is picturesque, but truly acceptable to the man or the woman prepared to accede to the great concept of a God Who can and does reveal Himself.

BACK TO VON DANIKEN: DID THE EPIC COME FROM SOUTH AMERICA?

But let us go back to the theories of Erich von Daniken, still as to the Epic of Gilgamesh. He suggests that the descendants of Gilgamesh might have brought the Epic with them from South America — thus explaining why there are similarities between the two cultures that are otherwise unexplained. For good measure, he even suggests the possibility that the Epic found its way into the library rooms of the Egyptian court where Moses would have had access to it! Von Daniken then summarizes:

> If we work on the hypothesis that the Epic of Gilgamesh came to Egypt from the Sumerians by way of the Assyrians and Babylonians, and that the young Moses found it there and adapted it for his own ends, then the Sumerian story of the Flood, and not the biblical one, would be the genuine account. (p. 69)

The logic is hard to follow, but perhaps two or three points should be noticed.

First, we have already seen that scholars accept that the Biblical account includes archaisms that indicate that it preceded the Babylonian and Assyrian versions of the Flood.

Secondly, a fragment of the Epic has been found at the Biblical city of Megiddo in Israel, and this pre-dated the copy from the palace of the Assyrian King Ashurbanipal by many hundreds of years. This was before the time of Moses, but not before Abraham. A far more realistic reconstruction, one that would not distort the known evidence, is that as this Epic was carried across the Fertile Crescent from Mesopotamia to Palestine, why could not a similar journey be true for the records in the early chapters of Genesis? In *that* way they could eventually come into the hands of Moses, brought into Egypt by the descendants of Abraham who had himself travelled that same Fertile Crescent.

FLOOD TRADITIONS WORLD-WIDE

Thirdly, flood traditions are known world-wide, and are often remarkably close to the Bible record. Robert T. Boyd has this telling summary:

"Is the Bible account of the great flood the only record known? There are no less than thirty-three separate racial records among people and races who are living today. Of this number, only the Egyptian and Scandinavian records fail to coincide absolutely with Moses' account. They differ in that their records attribute partial destruction to water and the rest by 'direct acts' of many gods. Greek tradition mentions a warning from gods that a great flood would be brought upon the earth because of man's wickedness, that an ark was built, that it rested on a high mountain, and that a dove was sent out twice. 'Fa-ha', whom the Chinese say is their founder, is represented as having escaped with his wife, three sons and three daughters from a flood that was sent 'because man rebelled against heaven'. The English, Hindus, Aztecs of Mexico, Incas of Peru, the Fiji Islanders, and even the American Indians have traditional stories about a flood (in "Tells, Tombs and Treasure," p. 72).

But before we leave the Flood, and the Epic of Gilgamesh, let us look at one more point relating to the viewpoint of Erich von Daniken. We have seen that he suggests that the Epic could have originated in South America — from the Tiahuanaco region (p. 69) — and we have referred to the fragment at Megiddo. But true writing is known in Peru only from about 500 A.D., though their culture was there about a thousand years earlier. But even if they immediately put their records into writing at the earlier date, this is still about a thousand years after the Epic of Gilgamesh was being carried across the Fertile Crescent, soon to find its way to Megiddo where it remained until its excavation in this generation.

THE CHARIOTS CRASH IN THE MOUNDS OF ANTIQUITY

Von Daniken makes another blunder as to the list on which the names of ten kings who lived "before the flood" are recorded. He lists the total reigns as coming to 456,000 years, then says:

> Periods of years that are quite incomprehensible to our way of thinking, although the names of all the rulers exist in long lists, neatly perpetuated on seals and coins. (p. 41)

This of course is the "Sumerian King List". We will not argue as to the figure of 456,000, though in checking two different sources we find the figure is 432,000. What we do challenge is that the names of these kings are "neatly perpetuated on seals and coins." The original list was actually eight kings — the Babylonian priest Berossos expanded it to ten. In 1923 an almost complete translation of the Sumerian original was published. However, it certainly did not come from "seals and coins", but from clay tablets. Cylinder seals were utilized by kings and others, with symbols associated with their own authority — it was on clay tablets that Sumerian records were kept. Coins were not minted until about 600 B.C. — making von Daniken 2,000 years or more out.

Thus the suggestion that the Epic was brought to Sumer from South America is totally unacceptable.

In any case, von Daniken himself has the Ark landing on Mt. Ararat (which by the way differs from the Epic of Gilgamesh — Mt. Ararat is the Biblical site). For his theory to be seriously considered would not the Ark have landed in South America? Another contradiction?

THE BOOK OF EXODUS FROM GILGAMESH!

Actually a lot more could be said about von Daniken's theories and interpretations relating to the Epic of Gilgamesh, and perhaps one other aspect should be noted. We have already seen that he suggests that the main thread of Gilgamesh runs parallel to Genesis, but a statement even harder to credit is at page 59:

> Or does the whole account in Exodus come from the Epic of Gilgamesh? Even that is possible.

The statement is virtually incredible! Exodus begins with the birth of Moses, and is a historical record of Israel as they became a nation. It certainly could NOT have come from the Babylonian Epic of Gilgamesh!

But our point is made. Another "chariot" has crashed into the mound of ancient Megiddo, where the earliest fragment of this ancient Epic was found. It is interesting to realize that this is the site of "Armageddon" — for "Har Megiddo" is "Mount Megiddo". Von Daniken is not the first — nor will he be the last — who has foundered when he presumed to attack that impregnable Rock of Holy Scripture.

CHAPTER 5

THAT "ATOMIC EXPLOSION" AT SODOM AND EZEKIEL'S SPACE VEHICLE

Years ago I was conducting an Exhibition for the Australian Institute of Archaeology in Adelaide, the capital city of South Australia. The series related to Biblical Archaeology, and the walls were decorated with suitable murals and charts, together with an impressive array of artefacts. Some were replicas, for of course many originals are simply not available even to a reputable institution. Others *were* originals, for the Institute has a magnificent collection of pottery and other artefacts recovered from various lands of the Bible.

One of the murals was a graphic display illustrating the destruction of the ancient cities of Sodom and Gomorrah — a reconstruction, to some extent based on the researches of the scientists of the Dead Sea Chemical Company that operates right in the area where the twin cities were supposed to be located.

I noticed a young man earnestly studying the mural, and then, as I moved around the room, he buttonholed me.

"You don't really expect me to believe all that do you?" He seemed half amused, half serious.

"Why not?" I responded, sizing him up.

"Well, I'm a science teacher — that story of the destruction is just a fanciful legend. No one with any scientific training would ever take it seriously."

"I'll tell you what," I said on a sudden impulse, "I'll make it the major subject of my lecture tonight — let me know what you think about it afterwards."

"Sure." He still smiled. "But you'll never convince me on that one."

So I lectured on the destruction of the twin cities, and afterwards my new friend admitted he was convinced on that particular point.

IMPOSSIBLE STORIES IN THE BIBLE?

"But there's lots of other impossible stories in the Bible," he countered. "Just because one turns out to be true it doesn't mean that all the others must be accepted. After all, truth IS sometimes stranger than fiction."

"Well, how about telling me another one of those unbelievable stories?" I suggested. This time it was the story of the crossing of the River Jordan in Joshua's day. As it happens, there are three recorded occasions when the river has been dammed up by a landfall at the same spot (the modern Damieh; Adam as it was in Joshua's day). Once again the young man was satisfied with the explanation, but was not prepared to consider the personal challenge of the Bible to his own life. That was another matter.

The main point of this story is that the Biblical description of the destruction of the cities of Sodom and Gomorrah can be substantiated by an acceptable reconstruction. This was not always so, for until relatively recent years it was quite unacceptable to all but the ardent Bible believer. It is relevant to note that Christ put His seal on its historicity (at Luke 17: 28-32).

CITIES IN THE SEA

One of the most important clues about these cities comes from the Bible, at Genesis 14: 3 where we have an interesting editing note. It refers to "the Vale of Siddim, which is the Salt Sea." "Which is the Salt Sea." If we accept the Bible at face value, that is an editing note to make the story clear to a later generation who no longer knew the area as a valley, but as part of the Dead Sea. Five cities are associated with the general area of this Valley, in that same chapter. Five streams once flowed into the southern part of the Dead Sea, probably being the major source of water for those five cities.

Hydrographers (water scientists) tell us that the southern half of the Dead Sea is relatively new — it is very much shallower than the northern half where the depths go to about 1,300 ft. Much of the southern part is only a fraction of that. Even in recent years the process of extension has continued — trees alongside the Dead Sea, photographed by the excavator Mervyn Kyle about 40 years ago, are now actually in the Dead Sea. Clearly it is to be expected that if cities once thrived in a valley area that has now been covered by the encroaching sea, they would hardly be visible after all this time.

The evidence supports this contention, for the Jewish historian Josephus and the Greek geographer Strabo both wrote about the ruins, still visible in their day. These men lived in the 1st Century A.D., and another pointer from their day is that a Roman road once crossed the Dead Sea in this area. It is still visible from the air — it goes to near the water's edge, then carries on again at the other side.

THE GEOLOGIST SPEAKS

Geologists tell us that there are great deposits of salt, sulphur and bitumen in the area, and also that the bubbles of natural gas which keep on escaping point to oil deposits.

The whole of this area is in the Great Rift Valley which extends from Mt. Hermon in the north right through to the Lakes system in Africa. At Dead Sea level this rift is 1,300 feet below the level of the Mediterranean Sea, and the northern part of the Dead Sea is yet another 1,300 feet deeper. Little wonder this rift is called "The Great Rift Valley".

Alongside the Dead Sea area there are great cracks, or "faults" as they are called by geologists, and consequently earth tremors take place there frequently.

Alongside the southern part of the Dead Sea is a mount called Jebel Usdum, which is Arabic for Mt. Sodom. The salt at its base is 150 feet deep over a distance of several miles. High up on this mountain there are clear evidences of a violent eruption, for the various strata of the earth's surface are found welded together as though by intense heat. It seems that the salt, the sulphur and the bitumen were hurled into the air when the great oil basin beneath these cities was disturbed, probably by an earthquake, and natural gases were ignited after they escaped into the atmosphere. The marl, as it is called, high up on Mt. Sodom is clear evidence of a violent eruption as great quantities of the earth's surface were hurled up the mountainside.

Another point is that the word translated "brimstone" actually means "bituminous material", and highly inflammable bitumen is very plentiful in the area. This is also referred to in the Bible, at Genesis 14 verse 10.

ARCHAEOLOGY ADDS ITS VOICE

Equally interesting is the testimony of archaeology.

In 1924 an expedition under Professor Mervyn Kyle found traces of a walled area at Bab-edh Dra'a, built by Canaanites about the time of Abraham. This was in one of the Moabite foothills, not far from Sodom and Gomorrah. Evidence was found that this had been a high place of worship to which people regularly came from their cities in the valley.

From about Abraham's time the site of this high place was no longer visited. We cannot say that this was the very time of the destruction of Sodom and Gomorrah — in fact, the pottery evidence suggests a time before Abraham witnessed the destruction of these cities of the plain. The point we DO make is that there had been people living in this valley which became the southern part of the Dead Sea. Sodom and Gomorrah were two of those cities whose people regularly would make pilgrimages — probably annually — to a site such as Bab-edh-Dra'a.

Similar evidence of civilisations dating to Abraham's day comes from the surface surveys of Professor Nelson Glueck in the general area alongside the Dead Sea. It appears the area had been inhabited spasmodically up to about the 19th century B.C., but was then not extensively settled again for several centuries. Some scholars see a possible link with the destruction recorded in Genesis chapter 19, in that trading and cultural centres were no longer situated in the water-covered "Vale of Siddim".

A SCIENTIFIC RECONSTRUCTION

Briefly then, it seems likely that at the time of this divine judgment an earthquake ground up rocks at the edge of the geological fault and natural gases from the underlying oil field carried many of these rocks, together with salt, sulphur and bitumen, high into the air. The natural gases ignited, and fire and bitumen literally rained from the sky.

WHAT ABOUT LOT'S WIFE?

But the question might be asked, what about Lot's wife? Do you really believe the story about the pillar of salt? The answer, of course, is yes. If people in Pompeii could be overcome by volcanic lava, why could not a woman fleeing from Sodom be overcome by rock salt? Pillars of salt are plentiful in the area, and one 40-foot pillar is known as "Lot's Wife". We do not suggest that this really does enclose Lot's wife, but it is evidence of a tradition that a woman was so enclosed. She certainly could have been, for the salt was 150 feet deep in this area — and this great layer of salt was fractured, with the other strata of the earth's surface, and hurled into the air.

In passing let us point out that Lot's wife did not simply glance over her shoulder. The word used implies a fixed staring. Her heart was still in Sodom and all she had left, even at this twelfth hour deliverance. In her heart Lot's wife was rejecting the grace of God, and she was overcome by the descending salt which encased her.

THE SMOKE, NOT THE FIRE

One delightful point of accuracy is seen at Genesis 19:28 which tells us that Abraham looked and saw the smoke ascending as the smoke of a furnace. Abraham was at Hebron, and there were mountain ridges in between Hebron and Sodom. He could not have seen the fire itself but he saw the smoke high in the sky. Abraham saw the smoke, we are told, and there is no mention of him seeing the fire. In this seemingly casual statement we are reminded of the eye-witness nature of these records.

Sodom and Gomorrah were cities of extreme wickedness, and their names have become by-words for depravity. The time had come when their "cup of iniquity" was full, and they met the judgment of God.

Just for a moment, let us go back to that verse about Abraham seeing the smoke ascending as the smoke of a furnace. The inherent meaning contains the idea of pressure — the result of many tons of earth pressing down on that hidden oil field.

NO ATOMIC BLAST AFTER ALL!

All this of course is in direct opposition to the theory of Erich von Daniken that the cities were destroyed by an atomic blast — for he suggests that a group of divers should investigate the Dead Sea "for radioactive traces of an atomic explosion over Sodom and Gomorrah" (p. 45).

He develops his hypothesis at some length, with the angelic messengers having to hurry Lot and his family out of the doomed city because the count-down had already begun (p. 53), with Lot's wife soon destroyed because of the effects of radiation when she looked back. According to von Daniken, "Lot's wife turned round and looked straight at the atomic sun. Nowadays no one is surprised that she fell dead on the spot" (p. 54).

In the last thirty years archaeological investigation has established what even non-Christians call "the substantial historicity" of the Old Testament records. Seemingly impossible stories have been found to be accurate after all — such as the two opposing temples in which the body and armour of Saul were placed at Bethshan; David's men coming along a tunnel to emerge inside the city of Jerusalem at the Pool of Siloam; this was not outside the city as was believed until the walls of David's time were uncovered by Dr Kathleen Kenyon in the early 1960's; the discovery that there was more than one Sanballat in history, vindicating the record in Nehemiah — and there are many others.

So what? The fact is, this old Book does not speak of an atomic explosion, even though Erich von Daniken has enough imagination to find one at Sodom. The reconstruction given above is perfectly acceptable "scientifically", and is compatible with the Bible record. Talk of an atomic explosion is merely begging the question.

Yet another "Chariot" has crashed, plunging into the salty waters of the southern half of the Dead Sea. It is virtually impossible to sink there — I tried and could not! Perhaps von Daniken's theory will float for a while, for on the surface it is plausible enough. And credulous people like plausible stories.

But let us move on to another hypothesis from "Chariots":

EZEKIEL'S SPACE VEHICLE

According to von Daniken, the "vehicle" that Ezekiel saw was a space chariot, and the gods "took him with them in their vehicle" (p. 57). But Ezekiel could not have been in touch with an almighty God, according to von Daniken, for "this kind of locomotion seems to me to be quite incompatible with the idea of an almighty God" (p. 57).

But again if we take the Bible record at face value we do not find the problem insuperable after all. In the very first verse of his prophecy Ezekiel says that he saw "visions from God". "Visions" are not necessarily literal phenomena, and in fact the descriptions that follow cannot all be taken literally in our physical sense. Ezekiel clearly shows that the "vehicle" moves in all directions at once (chapter 1, verse 17), and instead of this being one of von Daniken's "space chariots" it is in fact a symbolic presentation, telling us that he is in touch with that Transcendent One Who is not limited by space or gravity. He was not confined to a "space chariot", but was in fact above it (e.g. chapter 1, verse 25).

Ezekiel's prophecy includes a considerable amount of symbolic teaching, and even Ezekiel himself is told that he personally is a living symbol (Ezekiel 12:11) — he is a living symbol of the fact that the people are to go into exile, a prophecy which was literally fulfilled.

In view of the clear statements as to the symbolic elements and visionary method of this prophecy, there is little point in further following the outlandish interpretations given in "Chariots" as to the experiences of Ezekiel. Von Daniken's Ezekiel chariot crashes in the mists of a visionary hypothesis.

CHAPTER 6

OTHER GODS AND THEIR CHARIOTS

In chapter 6 of "Chariots" there is a virtual parade of deities as we are charioted swiftly from Eskimo mythology and Red Indian sagas to the Mayan ancestors of many of the people of Latin America. Chinese, African, Greek and Roman writings and religious "treasures" are all thrown in for good measure, as also arc modern anti-religious activities in Germany, and many others.

Clearly it cannot all be considered in this volume, but let us point out a few things which indicate the continuing approach of "Chariots".

THE MAYAN POPOL VUH

After telling us about Eskimo legends which claim that their first tribes were carried "by 'gods' with brazen wings", and of Red Indian sagas mentioning a thunderbird introducing fire and fruit to them, von Daniken goes on:

> Lastly, the Mayan legend, the Popol Vuh, tells us that the 'gods' were able to recognize everything: the universe, the four cardinal points of the compass and even the round shape of the earth. (p. 75)

It is relevant to mention that the extant version of the "Popol Vuh" contains a considerable amount of folk-lore — such as that about Zipacna, who killed 400 boys who then became the "Motz" group of stars (p. 101). It is said of Zipacna that "during the day he went about looking for food, and at night he carried mountains on his back" (p. 102).

So the authority now is the "Popol Vuh" — which is traditionally accepted as a sacred book of the Mayas of Central America. It is believed that the "book" became known after the conquest by the Spaniard Cortez, and was published in a Spanish form. However, the only copy today is in Latin. It is thought that the original would have been in pictographic form, somewhat resembling the Mexican codices — IF there was an original in writing. This view is put forward by some scholars (see e.g. "Sacred Books of the World," A. C. Bouquet, p. 82). It is possible that an original was destroyed at the time of the Conquest, but the relevant point is that it certainly is not good scholarship to quote such a work as though it were properly established as source material. This approach is seen all too often in "Chariots of the Gods?"

HINDU GODS AND CHARIOTS

Another example in the same chapter concerns Hindu religious writings. We learn concerning "this ancient Indian epic, the Mahabharata, . . . even at a conservative estimate its original core is at least 5,000 years old." (pp. 76-77)

Interesting. But certainly different from what A. C. Bouquet has to say in the volume already referred to:

> The second great Indian epic, the "Mahabharata," may be compared to the "Iliad" of Homer, in that it is the account of a war between two armed alliances, the Pandavas and the Kurus. (p. 227)

He goes on to say that its chief part is the famous "Gita," a didactic poem concerned with religious teaching. This is a comparatively late interpolation, and "as to date, it is placed by Radhakrishnan in the fifth century B.C." (p. 228). H. D. Lewis and R. L. Slater suggest that the famous "Gita," part of "The Mahabharata," probably dates to the third or fourth century B.C. (at p. 41 in "The Study of Religions," Pelican, 1966). It appears to have been worked over in later centuries, possibly receiving both Buddhist and Christian influences (pp. 228, 232). In any case, von Daniken says that "the oldest books of mankind" came from Ur (p. 40), and then says that about 2,000 B.C. the Sumerians (where Ur was) "began to record the glorious past of their people" (p. 40). Von Daniken is confusing when he talks of Indian writings "at least 5,000 years old." Are they older than the Ur writings? Which dates do we accept?

Although the early sources of much Hindu writing are lost in antiquity, scholars are cautious about giving dates that stretch back too far. A core that is "at least 5,000 years old" — as quoted above from von Daniken — is questionable to say the least. In fact, another story of a charioteer comes straight from the relatively late "Gita" itself in which—

> The scene is the great battlefield of Kurekshetra, the warrior is Arjuna and the companion to whom he puts his questions is the god, Krisna, who is the high god Visnu, come to Arjuna's aid in the human guise of his charioteer. ("The Study of Religions, p. 38.)

Another "Chariot of the Gods"! And Erich von Daniken tells us:

> And when Aryuna has found the gods after many perils, Indra, the lord of heaven, with his wife Sachi beside him, grants him a very exclusive audience. The two of them do not meet the valiant Aryuna just anywhere. They meet him in a heavenly war chariot and even invite him to travel in the sky with them. (p. 78)

(Note: Arjuna and Aryuna are alternative spellings.)

We find it hard to believe that von Daniken takes these legends and folk-lore so seriously. It is abundantly clear that much of such writings cannot possibly be taken as expresssions of literal fact in the sense that von Daniken accepts these "Chariots of the Gods". An example from this same "Gita" in the "Mahabharata" is where Arjuna exclaims that Krisna is the god of gods, and Krisna replies in part:

> "I am Visnu . . . I am Indra . . . I am Siva . . . I am the ocean . . . I am the Ganges River . . . I am the Ordainer (Creator) with faces in all directions . . . " ("The Study of Religions, p. 49.)

Arjuna is then given a vision of this great god who has many mouths, eyes, arms, thighs, feet, bellies and is "terrible with many tusks". Would this mean to von Daniken that this supreme Hindu deity is in fact an elephant?

THE EARTH ON A CROCODILE

Or to revert to the Mayan religion, would he accept their belief that the earth rested on the back of a crocodile? ("Civilization Past and Present," p. 597). Yet von Daniken insists — as shown above — that these people knew that the earth was round. How did the crocodile fit in? Perhaps there were enough to cover the four points of the compass.

As a matter of fact knowledge of a round earth was not restricted to the Mayas — one early indication being that in the 2nd century B.C. Ptolemy represented the earth as a curved surface (Civilization Past and Present, p. 608). In the Christian Gospels we find that Jesus referred to His own return to earth in such a way as to indicate that the earth was round — two women would be grinding, other people would be working in fields, while others would be in bed. These activities were

The pictures chosen illustrate various ancient "heavenly beings," chariots, and mythology. Similar "evidence" is used by Erich von Daniken to support his hypothesis of visits to earth by "astronaut-gods."

This line drawing is of the Egyptian Pharaoh Thutmose IV in battle with the Syrians (original in Cairo Museum).
Egyptian Pharaohs were supposed to be manifestations of the gods.
To the Egyptians, this WAS a "god in his chariot". Many of the symbols Erich von Daniken utilizes are distorted by his interpretations.

The original of this winged genius was in glazed brick in the palace of the Assyrian King Sargon. This was in the palace of the king referred to at Isaiah 20 — unknown until the recovery and excavation of the palace in the last century. The battle referred to by Isaiah was recorded on the palace walls.

This sphinx figure comes from the Assyrian city of Nimrud, dating to the 8th century B.C. Such winged figures are common Assyrian religious motifs.

The sirrush was a mystical symbol on the Ishtar Gate and Procession Way at Babylon. It is made up of three creatures, including the serpent. Erich von Daniken sees the snake as the "primaeval image of evil" (p. 127).

This cylinder seal impression shows Darius I of Persia and Babylon. The king is hunting, covered by the protecting symbol of Ahuramazda, ancient Persia's national god. It is a similar symbol to one which von Daniken interprets in his picture section as "an astronaut in a fiery chariot."

This human-headed bull figure was at Nimrud in ancient Assyria, dating to the 9th century B.C. (Or a five-legged astronaut complete with his wings?!!)

This 10th century B.C. design shows the Egyptian infant god Harpocrates coming into being from a lotus. Von Daniken utilizes such mythology as fact.

spread through the hours of the day and night, and hence required a round earth as this was the same event, at one time — His own return.

Another supposedly convincing fact quoted by von Daniken is that "the religious legends of the pre-Inca peoples say that the stars were inhabited and that the 'gods' came down to them from the constellation of the Pleiades." (p. 76) Do we also accept their belief that maize was the food of these gods who visited Central America? (Civilization Past and Present, p. 593.)

A LIMITED KNOWLEDGE OF THE MAYAS

Despite all the remarkable claims made for the Mayas, with their "incredible calculations" and inscriptions that "probably approach 400 million years" (p. 75), the fact is that

> "we probably know less about these South and Central American peoples than about any great civilization of the Old World. Most of our knowledge comes from archaeological research, recorded oral tradition, descriptions by early Spanish soldiers and priests, and the extraordinarily few surviving native records, such as three Mayan books of pictures and partially deciphered hieroglyphics" (Civilization Past and Present, p. 595).

This authoritative statement comes from a recognized text, authored by top American scholars — associated with Universities such as Southern California and Stanford. The body of editors is impressive, and this printing dates to 1969, the same year that von Daniken's book was published. While greater acceptance as experts and authorities does not necessarily mean that von Daniken is wrong, it is yet reasonable to ask that he substantiate his arguments, giving authorities where new information is submitted, and justifying dates and interpretations where these differ radically from those that are more traditionally accepted. Unfortunately von Daniken does not conform to such standards, but makes very many "new" statements that he simply does not substantiate.

To show how radically he disagrees with accepted scholarship we give one more brief quote from "Civilization Past and Present."

> The Mayas developed a remarkably accurate calendar and a sophisticated writing system based on hieroglyphics, but aside from dates almost nothing has been deciphered. . . .
>
> After about 900 A.D. the Mayas of northern Guatemala appear to have abandoned their stately temple centers or cities — for reasons as yet unknown. (p. 596)

The writer goes on to suggest a military invasion, and gives evidence of such activity with nearby peoples. Another possibility is also touched on in passing, for "disastrous droughts appear to have punctuated Mayan history. . . ." These authors certainly do not suggest visits from space-men that somehow led to the sites being deserted.

SIMILARITIES TO OTHER RELIGIONS

It is relevant to comment that there are interesting similarities to the religions of Babylonia, Assyria, and Egypt, just as von Daniken suggests (p. 76). These Mayas had a tradition about a world-wide flood that destroyed mankind, they had gods of the sky, the earth and the underworld, and human sacrifices were made to them. They had an amazing knowledge of astronomy, and even utilized observatories.

In these ways the Mayas showed great similarities to these other three nations of antiquity, but this is not really surprising. Through the centuries men have been fascinated by the movements of heavenly bodies, and there are many known cases of men making careful calculations based on their observations over long periods of time.

It is also thought-provoking to realize that these common traditions are at times somewhat similar to those in the first chapters of the Bible — up to the time of the confusion of man's language at Babel. There are archaeological writings about this incident, and it is no longer regarded as quite unbelievable. If men WERE scattered at that time, as the Bible declares, it stands to reason that they would take those early stories — of creation, the flood, long-living men, and the confusion of languages — with them, and this in fact is seen to be the case. However, it is also true that though there are similarities there are also great differences. Those traditions have become distorted as they have been handed on across the world. The Bible records are remarkably free of such corruption.

MOSES RESCUED AS A CHILD

This argument can be taken further as regards the theories of Erich von Daniken, in this same chapter 6. He tells of an Indian woman who put her child "in a little basket and put it in a river." (p. 78) He goes on to tell of a worthy man who fished the child out of the river and reared him. Then Erich von Daniken comments:

> Really a story that is hardly worth mentioning if it were not so remarkably like the story of Moses! (p. 78)

If we accepted von Daniken's date — supposedly "conservative" — of 5,000 years for this "Mahabharata" in which the story appears, this would imply that this incident was to be dated long before the time of Moses, and it would therefore throw doubt on the credibility of the Bible story. However, we have seen that scholars accept a date of about the 3rd century B.C. — about a thousand years AFTER Moses. If anything, the Indian legend is borrowed from the Bible, and not the reverse.

GODS BEGETTING MEN

We have said that von Daniken jumps from subject to subject, and this is again true at this point. Immediately after the reference to Moses he says:

> And, of course, there is yet another reference to the fertilisation of humans by gods. Like Gilgamesh, Aryuna, the hero of the Mahabharata, undertakes a long journey in order to seek the gods and ask them for weapons . . . (p. 78)

Here we have another "special" interpretation, a weaving together of a fabric of fact and fiction, of figures and symbols, and all presented authoritatively as though there was no other interpretation possible. If it were not that he uses illustrations from the Bible we would ignore the argument — and much of von Daniken's other points of discussion. But because Christians the world over will be offended, and even confused, by the "evidence" he assesses, some sort of a reply is called for. We refer of course to his comment concerning "the fertilisation of humans by gods".

Some of von Daniken's statements touching on this subject are now submitted, with relevant comments in passing.

> The gods of the dim past have left countless traces which we can read and decipher today for the first time . . . space travel, so topical today, was not a problem, but a reality, to the men of thousands of years ago. (p. 11)

A wild theory becomes fact! The "problem" is resolved, we "read" the traces left behind by the gods, space travel was a "reality" to men thousands of years ago. It is all so definite as von Daniken continues to put forward his insufficiently explained hypotheses as fact, then he moves to conclusions.

Non-sequiters abound.

> Even though I do not yet know who these extra-terrestrial intelligences were or from which planet they came, I nevertheless proclaim that these 'strangers' annihilated part of mankind existing at the time and produced a new, perhaps the first, homo sapiens. (p. 12)

At least the author acknowledges he does not know who they were or where they came from — yet if they have left those "countless traces" which "we can read and decipher today" it is strange that he has to make such an admission!

However, he is not short of ideas. At page 76 he has some of the gods coming "from the constellation of the Pleiades", while at pages 154 and 155 he speculates as to Martian visitors.

WHERE HOMO SAPIENS CAME FROM!

It is also a little hard to understand something else about von Daniken's god-men, his supposed first homo sapiens. At page 155 he takes his conjecture a step further as he suggests the possibility that his space visitors actually came from Mars — again establishing homo sapiens by interbreeding "with the semi-intelligent beings living there".

Then comes perhaps the strangest part. These new men, these giants who were god-men, "finally died out" (p. 155). Surely this would not be the fate of such a super-race? We would expect it to be the weaker, earth-bound mortals who would die out. But perhaps that would involve finding these god-men today, and unfortunately that is not so easy!

And at that same point von Daniken has these "giants who come from the stars" moving "enormous blocks of stone". But we have seen that written records and other evidence establishes conclusively that the Pyramids and those huge statues at Easter Island did not require the help of giants after all. Thus another chariot goes crashing in flames, carrying his giant astronaut-breeder-builder into the abyss of unsupported theories.

This certainly is a strange book. It goes on just three pages later (p. 158) to a discussion as to the problems of radio beams originating from intelligent beings in space. In that context von Daniken says:

> This realisation could mean a kind of coup de grace to the search for other living beings on the universe.

Strange. For we have been told of gods visiting us from outer space, and the author has "proclaimed" his view (see above) that these visitors interbred with mankind. Where do his contradictions end?

In challenging Christian beliefs von Daniken asks if "a single Christian" would be prepared "to recognise the god of the pre-Inca culture as the GENUINE god as the results of excavations in Peru?" (p. 73) We trust the answer is "No", for the evidence certainly does NOT warrant such a drastic conversion. But let us tie this also to the von Daniken doctrine of gods coming to earth and influencing future life:

> The religious legends of the pre-Inca peoples say that the stars were inhabited and that the "gods came down to them from the constellation of the Pleiades . . . and promised immortality to individual men . . ." (p. 76)

The promise of immortality is linked with fertilization by the gods, for von Daniken ties it in with the Epic of Gilgamesh which includes the Babylonian story of the Flood:

> We learn that Gilgamesh was a mixture of "god" and man — two-thirds "god", one-third man. Pilgrims who came to Uruk gazed up at him in fear and trembling because they had never seen his like for beauty and strength. In other words, the beginning of the narrative

contains the idea of inter-breeding between "god" and man yet again. (p. 64)

GODS CONDUCT BREEDING EXPERIMENTS WITH HUMANS

That is not all, for, according to von Daniken's theory, "it needed several experiments before men finally turned out as successfully as 'God' wanted" (p. 62) — but then another contradiction follows as the author says, "We could postulate that today we are similarly constituted to those fabulous unidentified beings." But he has stated that the race "finally died out" (see above) — though they were supposed to be homo sapiens, the name for man today.

Contradictions. Confusion. Where will it end? This book is disturbing, for many people have taken it very seriously.

And that leads to von Daniken's interpretation being applied to the Bible at this point. This present writing of an "alternative" to the "Chariots" is not meant only for a "Christian" circle of readers, and therefore it is difficult to explain that the Bible cannot be read and understood by everyone in the way that an ordinary novel can be understood. Spiritual writings demand spiritual language and spiritual understanding. The Bible is self-consistent as it presents doctrine and theology, but this self-consistency is not always readily apparent. It almost seems that God demands a point of faith before one can appreciate the marvels of the Book. To many who approach it with cynicism or a swaggering critical attitude that implies that God is rather fortunate to have such a person showing ANY interest, then the Book's treasures are simply not discovered. This Book of Spiritual values demands spiritual understanding. In fact, it calls for spiritual re-birth by the Spirit of God Who —

according to the Bible itself — is the ultimate Divine Author.

For the Christian, the claims of von Daniken as to gods fertilizing human stock with Divine seed are offensive, as well as being based on unacceptable exegesis. At page 51 he asks, "Where do the 'sons of God' come from?" and he goes on to quote Genesis 6:4 as to there being giants in the earth in those early days. He then states:

> Once again we have the sons of God, who interbreed with human beings. Here, too, we have the first mention of giants . . . What sort of creatures were they, these "giants"? Were they our forefathers, who built the gigantic buildings and effortlessly manhandled the monoliths, or were they technically skilled space travellers from another star?

WHAT THE BIBLE SAYS ABOUT SONS OF GOD

So let us examine the Bible at this point. First we notice that these "giants" are introduced literally thousands of years after Adam, who the Bible states was the first man. The word "giant" is used again in ordinary narrative parts of Scripture — one example being at Numbers 13:33, where it certainly does not refer to a breed who were part-god and part-human. Again, according to the Bible, two lines had developed in the history of man by this time, these being the Godly line of Seth and the ungodly line of Cain who killed his brother Abel, and went into "exile". The first human baby, according to the Bible, became a murderer.

Many Biblical scholars accept that "the sons of God" were the line of Seth and that a measure of inter-marriage took place with "the daughters of men" — the ungodly line of Cain. The statement "there were giants in the earth in those days" is simply a factual presentation, as with many other facts in this abbreviated history of thousands of years of the early history of mankind.

Were these giants "angels"? Again, if we accept the Bible's own teaching, Jesus said that they are without sex (at Matthew 22:30) and that when men enter into eternal life they too will not marry.

This teaching is radically different from that of von Daniken, who has representatives of homo sapiens taken off to another planet, with repeated breeding experiments, and any unfortunate results destroyed (pp. 71-72). And on the earth itself "A few specially selected women would be fertilised by the astronauts. Thus a new race would arise that skipped a stage in natural evolution." (p. 25)

What an imagination he has!

ENOCH IN A FIERY CHARIOT?

Again relating this to the Bible, von Daniken now refers to Enoch who, "according to tradition, disappeared for ever in a fiery heavenly chariot". (p. 61)

This adds considerably to the Bible account, which simply says,

> And Enoch walked with God: and he was not; for God took him (Genesis 5:24).

Where is the "fiery heavenly chariot"? The Bible makes as much reference to it as it does to the "flashing sparks" which von Daniken "seems to remember" often surrounded the Ark of the Covenant (pp. 58-59). No chariot is mentioned in the record of Enoch. This is a very disturbing, and even distressing, thing about "Chariots of the Gods?" It "seems to remember", and very often hypothesises imaginative theories as though they were fact. And in doing so it is laying an attack against that Book which is the treasured possession and guide to life for thousands upon thousands of people across the cultures of the world.

The Bible DOES require a faith commitment, and expects men to believe that there is one

Almighty God. But if that premise be accepted, there is no miracle or record in the Bible that is unacceptable to intelligent, thinking men and women. The miracles are demonstrations of the power of God, moral in content, often indeed one of the means by which the Divine lesson will be taught. On the contrary, the "miracles" of so many other peoples are either magic or legends that are so distorted that they are sources of amusement even to those who accept them as part of their own literature. The Bible stands alone, the unique revelation of Almighty God Who DID visit mankind in the Person of His Son, Jesus Christ.

And Jesus Christ has promised to return, another aspect which von Daniken seizes on as being a constant theme of the gods — astronauts — of old. But there is a difference, not the least being the descriptions and clues given as to the events to take place preceding that return. There is even a suggestion about "the elements melting with fervent heat" in the end time (2 Peter 3: 10). Coming events cast their shadows!

THE PROMISE OF THE REDEEMER'S RETURN

Prophecy is another subject, but just as surely as there were remarkable Old Testament prophecies fulfilled in Jesus (His birthplace, His public ministry in Galilee, His death by crucifixion, His resurrection and ascension), so the Christian believes that the "signs" point to His soon-return.

The Bible claims that Satan is at times transformed to be as an angel of light, deceiving if possible the very saints of God. We have already referred to this. As we compare the traditions and legends of old we very often find that there are half-truths, near-light, presentations that include some demonstrable facts, but including also interpretations that oppose belief in one Almighty God.

That Almighty God, in His wisdom, allows this so that the wheat is separated from the chaff, the sheep from the goats, the true searcher after God from the infidel.

But the evidence is sufficient for the earnest seeker, for, as Jesus Christ said,

> The Father seeketh such to worship Him (John 4:23).

God HAS come to earth — in the Person of His Son Jesus Christ. Men ARE taken to a realm beyond the earth, but not in a space ship or in bodies that need special helmets to prevent destruction by fire. Jesus Christ offers eternal life, and when that life is finally assumed in its fullness this corruptible must put on incorruption, this mortal must put on immortality.

That is the Christian hope, to be realized when Jesus Christ the Son of God returns. His promise is repeated at the very end of the Christian Bible, with the appropriate response of the Christian,

"Even so, come, Lord Jesus" (Rev. 22:20).

CHAPTER 7

HERE, THERE AND EVERYWHERE – AN ANCIENT MAP . . . VENUS . . . CARBON DATING

Anyone reading "Chariots of the Gods?" soon finds that the author jumps from subject to subject, culture to culture, extravagant claim to unsupported conclusions. His writing is something of a literary maze. Thus a systematic analysis of his work is difficult, and even impossible if it must be confined to a small book. In this chapter we consider a number of subjects as we briefly explain why we reject his hypothesis at particular points.

PIRI REIS AND THAT ANCIENT MAP OF THE WORLD

The author of "Chariots" uses some ancient maps to bolster his hypotheses as to the visits of gods from space. These maps had been the property of a Turkish naval officer, Admiral Piri Reis. One map especially was seized on, for it was supposed to be part of a map of the world taken from a very great height (p. 30). According to von Daniken, this 16th century map was virtually identical with one taken from a space-ship hovering over Cairo. To prove his point, the map is included in "Chariots", together with other pictures in the central part of the book. It takes some effort to be able to fit the Piri Reis map onto the one taken over Cairo, and, as von Daniken himself states, the various countries must be re-shuffled to make them fit (p. 29). But having done this preliminary juggling they are, he claims, "fantastically accurate" (p. 30). The explanation put forward by the author of "Chariots" is that they must have been taken from a high-flying aircraft or from a space-ship (p. 31).

But Piri Reis himself stated on the map in question that he had consulted 20 different earlier charts in the preparation of his own work. These were maps that ranged over approximately two thousand years of time. One interesting sidelight is that in fact the River Amazon is shown twice on the Admiral's map, this probably being explained by the fact that it WAS a piecing together of a number of charts, meticulously drawn but still coming from widely differing sources.

In any case, though the map is indeed a remarkable achievement of the Renaissance period, it is not as accurate as is claimed by von Daniken. Nearly a thousand miles of coastland is missing from the east side of South America, and Antarctica is a landmass joined directly to South America — the ocean between is ignored. A space photograph certainly would not produce such a result. Nor would it have made a total error of about 5% in the size of the land masses.

The Piri Reis work is highly creditable, being a painstaking attempt to correct the known efforts of the cartographers before him. We do well to accept his own statement that he consulted 20 other charts in the preparation of this new map — but he did NOT take a journey in a space ship!

WERE "ANIMAL GODS" WORSHIPPED AND EATEN?

All the gods who are depicted in cave drawings in Sweden and Norway have uniform undefinable heads. The archaeologists say that they are animal heads. Yet isn't

there something rather absurd about worshipping a "god" whom one also slaughters and eats? (p. 49)

Whether it is absurd or not, it is fact. Ancient Egyptians worshipped bulls and other animals, as well as edible birds and fish which were the symbols of various gods. The Canaanites, the Babylonians, the Assyrians — they all revered the bull but this did not prevent them feasting on it.

FURNACES WITH AIR CHANNELS AT EZION-GEBER

Erich von Daniken has Ezion-Geber spelt as "Ezeon Geber" (p. 62), and refers to the earlier held view that buildings there were smelting installations "consisting of a regular ultra-modern furnace with a system of air channels, chimney flues and openings for specific purposes."

The archaeologists whom he brands as inflexible have long ago recognized that these "smelting installations" were in fact store rooms. Smelting did take place in the area, but the particular interpretation as to the controlled air channels, put out by Professor Nelson Glueck, has been withdrawn. The author of "Chariots" is not up to date at this point; nor is he accurate when he says that "All these finds are estimated to be at least 5,000 years old!" (p. 62) Some were dated to about 1000 B.C. — approximately 3,000 years ago.

Nor is copper sulphate that from which copper is obtained — it comes from sulphide minerals. But perhaps these space charioteers, with their advanced techniques, had missed out on learning this particular one?

In passing it is worth pointing out that this is another clear example of archaeologists being prepared to meet the facts and to change strongly-held viewpoints, as was the case with this widely-publicized theory. This hardly fits the cynical approach of von Daniken against archaeologists.

A FIREBALL IN 1500 B.C.

Sometimes the points that von Daniken brings up are so weak as supports to his argument that one feels like saying, "So what?" One such case is that of a text from the time of the Egyptian Pharaoh Tuthmosis III, telling of a ball of fire with an evil smell — the Pharaoh and his men watched it until it rose in a southerly direction and disappeared from view. (p. 80)

A fireball was witnessed by several members of the Church of which I was a member in Malvern, Victoria, Australia. It came through the ceiling, roared through the church, then disappeared through a window. Was it the exhaust of a space chariot? Of course not! But if imagination is allowed to run riot there could be a terrific story to tell. The point is, a report from a credulous Egyptian back in ancient days is hardly sufficient evidence to substantiate a visit from a space craft.

THOSE ANCIENT WATER TUNNELS

At page 36 he tells us about water tunnels at Tiahuanaco, constructed with "such precision that our modern concrete conduits seem the work of mere bunglers in comparison".

This sort of statement is supposed to impress on us that only technicians with the sort of know-how associated with visitors from space could have made them.

The argument is again quite unconvincing. Anybody who has waded through that amazing conduit of Hezekiah underneath the walls of ancient Jerusalem — as I have done — must acknowledge that some of these men of old had great technical know-how to construct their extensive conduits.

The ruins of the one built by Herod the Great from Mount Carmel to the sea are still amazing — it was a "double-header" — two tunnels, one on top of the other. The ruins can be seen at Caesarea.

But Herod and Hezekiah certainly did not claim the help of astronauts for the building of these ancient marvels.

DID THE WORLD REALLY FLOAT ON AN ELEPHANT?

One of the drawings opposite page 97 of "Chariots" shows a man in some sort of a vessel, with others outside, possibly in an attitude of worship. The structure is borne up by two men who are in turn on the back of an animal that looks like an elongated cat. We are not told the significance, as it is simply included with "More ancient drawings — from Navoy". Possibly it is meant to convey the idea that a visitor from outer space came in such a vessel, for what looks like the rays of the sun surround it and two of the other pictures on the page speak about men in space suits.

One Hindu story told of the world being held in place on the back of a huge elephant (plus a tortoise, etc.). If such drawings as this opposite page 97 are to be used as serious argument it is reasonable to assume that the elephant story must also be taken seriously.

THE TEACHING OF A SIMPLE LANGUAGE

At page 26 we learn of people using their "simple language" to put in saga form that the gods had visited them.

There is no such thing as a simple language. Linguists of this generation have established that all languages are very complex. Earlier generations had thought that primitive peoples would have simple languages, but this has not proved to be the case. The complexities of human language are great whether one is dealing with "educated" people or those who know little of modern civilization.

Written forms of communication have developed from simpler to more complex forms, but this is not so with speech. And according to von Daniken those primitive people were able to pass on the details of the visit from space (p. 82). They understood the language of the gods, and believed their promise of a return (p. 103). They are supposed to have known that "the body cells (can) continue to live, slowed down a billionfold after special treatment" (p. 105).

Not only were these people possessed of — apparently — a very complex language, but they had knowledge we are only now beginning to rediscover. These were not the simple people von Daniken hypothesises! They appear rather to have been transported by some time machine into the 21st century A.D.

VENUS AND VON DANIKEN

It is commonplace that many enthusiasts thought that life might exist on the planet Venus but, as von Daniken himself acknowledges (p. 151), that theory is no longer held because of the very high temperatures on its surface.

However, our special interest in von Daniken's theory is that he discusses the viewpoint of Dr Emanuel Velikovsky in "Worlds in Collision" — which we are not discussing except insofar as it is relevant to this analysis. Von Daniken states that Velikovsky's theory as to the formation of Venus is confirmed by the results from the space-craft Mariner II. As Velikovsky associates this with the action that caused the Red Sea to open when the Israelites crossed it in the days of Moses, it follows that Venus could not have been in existence until less than three and a half thousand years ago.

The relevance to von Daniken is that elsewhere he makes the following statement:

> In the mountainous Asian region of Kohistan a cave drawing reproduces the exact position of the constellations as they actually were 10,000 years ago. Venus and the earth are joined by lines. (p. 43)

So which IS true? If Venus was formed 3 to 4 thousand years ago it certainly was not there 10,000 years ago. This seems to be yet another contradiction.

"THEY WILL NEVER BE ON SHOW IN A MUSEUM"

So says von Daniken at p. 117, referring to the huge colossi of the Olmecs of Mexico. "No bridge in the country could stand the weight," he tells us.

Gordon Whittaker (in "Some Trust in Chariots", Ed. E. W. Castle and B. B. Thiering, Westbrooks Pty. Ltd., Perth and Sydney, Australia, p. 51) points out that some of these giant heads ARE found in museums, and that "one was recently transported thousands of miles to the Metropolitan Museum of Art in New York for a special exhibition." Whittaker is an authority on Aztec culture. He goes on to defuse a whole series of "Chariot" myths, one other interesting example being that of von Daniken's helmeted spacemen at the Toltec capital. These actually are Toltec soldiers wearing headdresses and protective breastplates. Their "communications equipment" are nothing more than spear throwers.

THAT CLOTH FROM HELWAN

Another von Daniken "evidence" of visitors from outer space is that at Helwan there is a piece of cloth with fabric so fine that today it could only be woven "in a special factory with great technical know-how and experience" (p. 43).

Equally impressive woven fabrics are known much earlier, as text-books and museums make clear. Not only have beautifully woven fabrics come down to us many centuries older than this particular cloth, but even some of the ancient looms have been preserved for posterity. Von Daniken's sensationalism is again unjustified.

THE SO-CALLED "ELEPHANT ISLAND" IN THE RIVER NILE

A lady who read the first edition of "Crash Go The Chariots" commented — "It's convincing — but I'd still like to know about the 'elephant shaped island'." I had not thought it specially significant, but others also might ask questions, so here is a comment.

Von Daniken states that even in the older texts this island in the middle of the Nile was called "Elephantine" because it always resembled an elephant and he asks, "But how did the ancient Egyptians know that, because this shape can only be recognised from an aeroplane at a great height?" (p. 85).

However, the Greek word "elephantinos" does not mean "elephant", but "ivory". It is itself a translation of the Egyptian word "Yeb", and the island of Yeb is known before the times of the Greeks, who called it "Elephantine".

Secondly the island does not resemble the shape of an elephant today, as is implied in "Chariots". And even if it did (which the maps negate), this would argue more against von Daniken's claim than for it, in that relatively small river islands tend to change their shape over long periods of time.

RADIO CARBON DATING

A subject touched on briefly by Erich von Daniken is radio carbon dating.

The theory is not now as "popular" as it was, and dating by this and similar methods has become suspect. When carbon dating was first announced by Dr Libby in 1949 it was thought to be the last word, but that early confidence has been replaced by a sense of caution.

Carbon dating can be shown to be relatively accurate for one half-life — that is, approximately five and a half thousand years — for there are written records that can be put alongside dates for that time period. Beyond that period dating is an open question for there simply are not absolutes against which specific dates can be fixed with accuracy.

Thus it is not surprising to find how dates vary, and sometimes the estimates range very widely.

Confusion again! Von Daniken (p. 110) refers to "the omnipotent carbon isotope C 14", and is content to accept that carbon dating is accurate, for he uses it to give a comparison with a date relating to Egypt. Actually his comparison can easily be shown to be not valid, for the figures he quotes as agreeing "pretty well" with those given by ancient Egyptian priests work out to be over 3,000 years more than the 10,400 he quotes. His own mathematics can be challenged, but the point we are making is that he accepts Carbon 14 as a dating method when he wants to "establish" his case.

Yet we go over two pages (to page 112) and we find ourselves further confused by his seemingly contradictory statements. We quote:

> Our hitherto existing methods of dating, including the famous carbon isotope C 14, which makes everyone so happy, leave great gaps as soon as we come to an age of more than 45,600 years.

"EVERYONE HAPPY" or "UNRELIABLE"

We have already commented on the accepted fact that there are no "absolutes" for comparison beyond one half life of approximately five and a half thousand years. However, we read that von Daniken says that this dating method "makes everyone so happy". But what ARE we to believe? On the same page he says, "Even recognised scholars have told me that they considered the C 14 method rather unreliable . . ." and "These critical voices should only be accepted with limitations . . ."

We, too, have reservations about carbon dating — as do many scholars — and to that extent agree with von Daniken. But is it a satisfactory method of research to accept its evidence when the figures are apparently in agreement with a theory, but to accept it at other points only with limitations? And is it logical argument to say it "makes everyone happy" and then immediately — in the same paragraph — to state that "recognised scholars" have told him that they consider the method unreliable?

It would seem that von Daniken is selective in the presentation of his arguments — a method is acceptable or unacceptable according to whether it fits the preconceived theory. Scientific investigation, and the research methods of modern academic inquiry, demand that ALL evidence be examined impartially. A method cannot be recommended or utilized at one point and then rejected if it happens not to fit a preconceived notion or hypothesis.

Let me illustrate. When I took out my Ph.D., I wrote a thesis which involved certain tests spread over a considerable time. I thought I knew what the results would be, but it all had to be outlined very clearly in the "Prospectus" before ever I had run those tests. My supervising Professors (at the University of South Carolina in Columbia) were extremely careful to see that my procedures were logically followed step by step, that there was no "cooking" the results to suit any hypothesis. The procedures had to be consistent, with an approach that was not prejudiced or biased.

But let us return to carbon dating — if, according to von Daniken, it "makes everyone happy", then why are "recognized scholars" criticizing it because it is "unreliable"? They would hardly be shouting with glee over something they consider should be approached with caution!

DAVID'S FIGHT WITH A 6-FINGERED GIANT

Von Daniken suggests the need to "query our Old Testament dating" (p. 59) because of the incident recorded at II Samuel chapter 21 where David fights with a giant who had six fingers and six toes.

We quote from "The Wycliffe Bible Commentary", at p. 304:

> "Six fingers . . . six toes" — This was not an unusual deformity in ancient times, nor is it in modern times. Pliny mentioned such a peculiarity in his "Natural History". According to Leviticus 21: 18 one with such a deformity was excluded from the temple service.

Years ago I was lecturing on this part of the Old Testament at the Melbourne Bible Institute in Australia. I had gone to the trouble of "digging in" in researching this incident, and had even come up with the interesting fact that one of the kings of England had the same deformity. I must have seemed a little defensive to some members of the class, for suddenly I noticed a hand go up — a very courteous young lady! She was a fully qualified nursing sister. I stopped, and asked what she wanted.

"My sister was born with six toes on both feet."

This condition is relatively common today. There is no problem as to this fact of Bible history.

ABOUT THE DEAD SEA SCROLLS

It is also relevant to point out that yet another von Daniken inaccuracy is seen in his reference to *The Apocalypse of Moses* at p. 60. He refers to this among "hitherto unknown texts" before the recent finding of the Dead Sea Scrolls. However, this particular text has been widely known for several centuries, and is typical of the documents put out by Jewish writers about the time of the New Testament. Such "pseudepigraphic" writings took the name of a recognized authority in order to gain greater acceptance. Scholars do NOT regard *The Apocalypse of Moses* as serious history, nor do they regard it as genuinely coming from the hand of Moses.

In the same context von Daniken brings two scrolls together, though he uses the name of only one — the so-called *Lamech Scroll*, an erroneous title which scholars have long since discarded in favor of *The Genesis Apocryphon*. Von Daniken brings together part of this writing and the pseudepigraphic *Book of Enoch* and speaks of "the astonishing . . . information" (p. 61) told to Noah's parents about the coming flood. But both these writings are known to date to approximately New Testament times — and many such writings can be pointed to, claiming to come from great men of the past in an attempt to gain greater favor for them. We certainly do not have here new "information" given to Noah.

From none of these Dead Sea scholls does von Daniken produce genuinely new evidence. He continues to confuse issues by combining fact with distortion as he attempts to bolster his own predetermined hypotheses. Much of the material to which von Daniken refers at this point is in the same category, and is certainly not in the same class as Genesis for being accepted as fact.

THE INDIAN PILLAR THAT DOES NOT RUST

Von Daniken publishes a picture of an old Indian pillar in the centre section of his book. The caption tells us that the iron in this pillar does not rust, and that the pillar is hundreds of years old.

This pillar is situated at Delhi and the story of its "special" qualities is well-known. It is regarded by many people as a lucky charm, and some scholars suggest that the constant placing of sweaty hands on its sides helps to prevent rust. However (despite von Daniken's claim to the contrary at page 44), it is NOT rust-proof, for it does contain phosphorus and does show signs of some rust though it is true that it is remarkably well-preserved. Such a phenomenon does not, however, point to some special technique introduced by astronaut gods, any more than the fact that there were other techniques known to ancient people would surprise modern scholars.

Let me illustrate. In the days of my association with the Australian Institute of Archaeology we welcomed into our collection an original bronze figure of the god Baal. It had a leg missing, and we had a modern one added. The metal men told us the original was harder than they could make — to their surprise.

There are many other examples of advanced techniques being known to people of long ago — witness the magnificent gold vessels from Ur, dating to about 2,500 B.C. But their two-storeyed houses also surprised the excavators. This in no way suggests a visit from space, but simply indicates that technical knowledge was more advanced than we of the 20th century would have expected.

The famous iron pillar to which von Daniken refers is in the same category.

CHAPTER 8

SPIRITUAL FORCES AROUND US

EDGAR CAYCE AND THOSE UNEXPLAINED MEDICAL PRESCRIPTIONS

The story of Edgar Cayce reads very easily in "Chariots" — a young man in a coma suddenly spoke clearly, prescribing the right medicines for his own recovery. Soon he was giving two consultations a day, in the presence of doctors, always in a trance. His diagnoses and prescriptions were accurate, but he could not remember what he had said when he came out of the coma. Cayce died in 1945.

Von Daniken attributes Cayce's strange powers to some form of extra-sensory perception, and advocates research to further tap the unknown resources of the human brain (p. 163). He tells of important advances in the parapsychological departments of many important universities (p. 160).

We do not rule out the possibility of extra-sensory perception: in fact, the evidence is very strong that at times mind has strange powers over matter. There are some people who can accurately call the side on which a coin will fall more often than can be accounted for by chance. Various other properly controlled experiments have indicated that there are people with "special" powers, able to exercise some measure of control over material things without physical contact.

This is not surprising if we accept the Bible's point of view, for we learn there that man is made in the image of God. We are "introduced" to God in Genesis chapter 1, the first chapter of the Bible, and there we read of God speaking and material results following as the objects and creatures of the world come into being. At Hebrews 11:3 we learn that the things we now see did not originally come from visible things. The Great Infinite God is Spirit, as Jesus reminded us (John 4:24), unable to be contained in or by material things. God created man in His own image — and thus latent powers whereby mind is shown to be superior to matter do not altogether surprise us. Most of us know the experience of thinking of someone we have not heard of or thought of for years, then seeing that person "in the flesh" — and other similar experiences. Perhaps part of the explanation is that man is not only "matter" but is in fact made in the image of God Who is Spirit, the One Who "spoke and it was done".

But let us also be bold enough — and honest enough — to say that perhaps there is another answer. We are surrounded by spiritual forces, powers we cannot altogether dismiss lightly as sheer imagination or hallucinations.

If this be accepted, it becomes entirely possible that Edgar Cayce was controlled by some spiritual force outside himself. I have a tape in my possession in which an interviewer talks to several people who claim to "speak in tongues".

Some of those interviewed seemed to have some sort of genuine experience, but there were others who undoubtedly were possessed by what would generally be called "evil spirits". At times they did physical damage to those whom they possessed, and could be violent in their responses to the interviewer.

Let us think of another illustration. One of my friends in Fiji dabbled with a form of spiritism, but he gave it up — permanently I hope — because he found that it was not uncommon for an evil spirit to try to drive the one it possessed to a violent death. I do not profess to understand this altogether but my friend was a highly qualified Government official and I have no reason to doubt some of the strange experiences of which he told me.

FIRE WALKERS IN FIJI

The argument can be developed in another way. I have had a number of visits to Fiji, and lived there for some time. On one occasion I went with a group of friends to watch the fire walking by the Indians, just a few miles out of Suva. It was eerie to say the least. Not only did they walk on absolutely red hot coals, but they danced up and down on them as though they were thoroughly enjoying the experience. I walked over next to the raised mound of ashes to make sure they really were hot — I had to put my hand up against my face to shield my eyes from the rising steam.

That was not all.

Many of these "priests" had iron skewers right through their bodies — through their mouths, extending from one side of the cheek to the other, through their stomachs, through their necks, through their arms, through their legs. And with all these extras in their bodies they marched several miles to the site of the red-hot coals.

When the ceremony was all over I watched as the skewers were taken out by an elderly priest in a little flower-bedecked "temple". Then a yellow powder — said to be the "magic" tamarisk — was sprinkled where the skewers had been, and there was no sign whatever of blood.

At the time I was in charge of the reporting of the Legislative Council debates in Suva, and the next morning I was working away in my office when an Indian carpenter came to repair a window. I was surprised to recognize him as the leader of yesterday's fire walkers — the young man who had carried a large idol object that looked like a bird in a cage, to the place of their sacred ceremony.

I asked him to show me his bare feet, and he willingly complied.

"How come your feet are not burned?" I asked.

"Govindra gives me power," he answered in reasonable English. Govindra was his particular deity.

"Did you treat your feet with some special oil or ointment before you walked on the hot coals?" I asked.

"No — Govindra would not let my feet be burned when my faith is strong."

One of these fire-walkers had his stomach cut open with a knife, and it was then healed over by a Hindu priest — to all intents and purposes the healing seemed to be complete, though — as photographic evidence verified — his stomach certainly was opened.

"How do you explain all these strange things that you can do to your bodies?" I had to repeat myself to the carpenter-priest, making my meaning clear. But the answer was clear enough.

"Govindra protects us. There is no problem."

No problem. I told this Indian carpenter about the Carpenter Whom I followed, Jesus Who had come to give mankind new life. His interest was only that of politeness. Govindra claimed his allegiance.

Another one of the "lesser lights" among the fire-walkers worked in the Law Department, just across the corridor. Later that day I looked carefully for the signs of scars where the skewers had been forced right through his cheek. On either side, where the penetration had been made, there was just the smallest little black spot. Because I knew him I had watched carefully the previous day as the skewers were pulled out — no bleeding.

EVIL SPIRIT POWERS

We include this story in "Crash Go the Chariots!" to make the point that there are spiritual powers which defy explanation in materialistic terms. I could tell of other personal experiences which are equally baffling — as when a group of young people practising one of the simpler forms of black magic were able to tell me my wife's name (Avis — she was not with me, nor was she known to them), and they went on to other details which they could not have known. The thought came to me that, unknown to them, this "revelation" was possible because of contact with evil spirit powers, and, because I am a Christian, I prayed. My words were something like this:

"Lord Jesus, if this thing is evil, let it stop right now."

From that moment those young people could not tell me any more, not even to complete the word they were in the process of spelling out. And in the three weeks that I was staying in that Fijian house they could never "communicate" at any time that I was present in the room where they were so engaged. They came to associate me with the blockage, for they could manage quite well when I was not present. They would laughingly say, "Hey man, you must be a Jonah!"

I have had similar unexplainable experiences in India, where I lived for two years. And my time in the United States has made it abundantly clear that black magic, Satan worship, contacts and experiences with evil powers, are relatively commonplace.

One of my former students is Rick Carreno, previously a leader of the Hell's Angels in Los Angeles. In private conversations, after his conversion, and in public testimony, I have heard him tell almost unbelievable things about the abominations associated with black magic and Satan worship. The fact of evil spirit powers is all too well attested.

So we are not challenging Erich von Daniken's argument that there are, and have been through the centuries, beings commonly called "gods".

WHAT THE BIBLE TEACHES

Nor does the Bible reject such a concept, though it is very clear in its statements that the "gods" of the nations are not true gods at all, but are powerless before the might of the true God, Yahweh — Jehovah as we English-speaking people pronounce the name. When I was Editor of "Buried History", the quarterly journal issued by the Australian Institute of Archaeology, I wrote an article which I called "The Plagues of Egypt". It was reprinted as a booklet (and is still available) — it was very well received by a large reading public.

This was virtually an exposition of a verse in the Bible, at Exodus 12: 12 — "Against all the gods of Egypt I will execute judgment." It went through the ten judgments just before the Israelites were delivered from their Egyptian slavery, and showed that every one of them could be linked in a special way with the leading gods of Egypt. Ra the sun god had his eye darkened at the time of the thick darkness, the judgment on the Nile showed just how powerless Osiris the god of the Nile was, the thousands upon thousands of frogs made it clear that Heqt, the frog-headed goddess of fertility, could not even control the fertility of frogs.

The Bible recognizes that there are other "gods". It does not explain their origin in great detail but does tell us of a rebellion in the heavens against the authority of almighty God.

In addition, the Bible gives a clue as to the origin of "gods" who developed from men — that is, men whose prowess was such that legends grew about them until they were deified. We refer to Genesis chapter 10, the so-called "Table of the Nations". I quote from another book of which I am author, "In the Beginning God . . ." at page 109:

Question: *Is this document known as "The Table of the Nations" in Genesis chapter 10 accurate in its presentation of history?*

Answer: The table itself is astonishingly accurate, according to Professor W. F. Albright, recognized as one of the greatest authorities on archaeology the world has seen. He says (in "Recent Discoveries in Bible Lands," p. 70 ff):

> "It stands absolutely alone in ancient literature without a remote parallel even among the Greeks . . . 'The Table of Nations' remains an astonishingly accurate document . . . (It) shows such remarkably 'modern' understanding of the ethnic and linguistic situation in the modern world, in spite of all its complexity, that scholars never fail to be impressed with the author's knowledge of the subject."

Archaeology has given clear testimony to the accuracy of the chapter, for nearly all the names mentioned are now known. Once again, the Bible records have been substantiated in no uncertain manner — not only as regards the people who are in the centre of Biblical history, but as regards many other peoples as well. The Assyrians, the Medes, the Greeks, the Egyptians and many others are referred to, and referred to in many ways that are, again, astonishingly accurate. We even find mention of points that were long ago forgotten, but are now known to have been just as the Bible briefly states. One example is that Nineveh was established by the rulers of Babylon, stated in Genesis chapter 10, verses 1 and 12. This is quite in harmony with what the monuments tell us.

This chapter tells us of Nimrod, who "began to be a mighty hunter before the Lord" (verse 9), and Asshur, who first built Nineveh (verse 11). Both these men of renown were later worshipped as gods. This practice is seen with many of the gods of antiquity, especially in the Greek and Roman periods — witness the so-called "Olympian gods".

MEN WHO BECAME GODS

The Olympian gods were supposed to be concerned intimately with mankind, ready to help and encourage that which was good and to banish that which was foolish or vainglorious. It seems that originally they were men possessed of vast power and energy, but when they "became" gods it was at the same time recognized that they were imperfect and finite. Though possessed of great strength they were not almighty, and though "deathless" they were not in the true sense eternal. They were rather different from the astral gods, such as Helios the sun god and Selene the moon goddess, who moved in their own courses and were virtually indifferent to the affairs of men.

In the Homeric age, each deity was thought of as having a separate house, magnificently designed and furnished. If the gods came like bolts of lightning from the sky there would be worthy houses for them — thus Zeus had his temple at Olympia, Athene had the Parthenon in Athens, while Apollo could reside at Delphi — and of course each had other smaller houses in different places. The good god Hermes and the bad god Ares had smaller houses because they were each thought of as being always on the move.

A GOD WHO SWALLOWED HIS CHILDREN

Zeus was the god of the sky and the weather, and about 600 B.C. he was conceived by the Greeks as either the sky itself or as the great being that lived in the sky, and so was responsible for the weather. He was supposed to live on the summit of Mt. Olympus, the highest point in Greece. But where did he come from?

Unlike the religion of Judaism and Christianity, the Greeks told of the origin of their "creator" god, Zeus. The god Kronos swallowed all his own children by the goddess Rhea (his own sister), except for his youngest child Zeus — he swallowed a stone instead of this child, who was hidden in a cave in Crete and looked after by animals and protected by armed spirits. Zeus soon forced Kronos to vomit forth his brothers and sisters, and a great "battle of the gods and giants" took place. Then began Zeus' visits to men and women.

How different all this is from the majestic concept of Jehovah, Whose character is presented in the Scriptures!

The Greek idea was to worship the god through a statue because in this way he was praising his god. In a sense this was anthropomorphic religion — gods represented in human form — in that the Greeks were suggesting that the athlete was the nearest that humans came to physical perfection, and so was nearest to their gods. As we have seen, in a sense this was tied to their "humanism", for to them gods were ideal human beings. So they thought of Zeus as a divine athlete, and as such he was presented naked — for it became the practice for athletes to run unclothed. Zeus was the prototype of mankind, created in a perfect image of mankind. Thus Homer did not look on men as created in the image of God, but rather he looked on the gods as made in the likeness of men.

THE HUMAN BODY "DEIFIED"

Zeus as the "creator" who loved mankind had to be depicted as an ideal man, physically perfect. This "worship" of the human body is seen in the very manner of Greek dating. Christians date their calendar from the "Year of our Lord" and the Romans from the foundation of the city, but the Greeks of old thought in terms of the first Olympiad — actually 776 B.C. An Olympiad was the period of four years between one religio-athletic festival and the next held at Olympia.

Referring to this new approach to athletic prowess Charles Seltman says:

> "The institution of organised athletics as an act of worship towards Zeus, and of the body trained to perfection as a thing dedicated to God, was a new and most startling concept in the history of mankind. But it was the necessary prelude to the birth of humanism." ("The Twelve Olympians," p. 40.)

VON DANIKEN RECOGNIZES THAT MEN "BECAME" GODS

This is relevant to the concepts put forward by Erich von Daniken. He recognizes this principle of gods being deified, as when he tells of the origin of Im-Hotep, the Egyptian god of medicine. We quote:

> The ground plan (of a building "of supernatural origin" — Ed.) was drawn by the deified being Im-Hotep. Now this Im-Hotep was a very mysterious and clever personality — the Einstein of his time. He was priest, scribe, doctor, architect and philosopher rolled into one . . . the brilliant Im-Hotep built the step pyramid of Sakkara for his king, who was called Zoser . . . The structure . . . was called

> the "House of Eternity" by Im-Hotep. He had himself buried in it, so that the gods could wake him on their return. (p. 85)

As we say, it is somewhat similar to the legends about the gods of Greece and Rome, but von Daniken has that something which is specially selected, such as "that the gods could wake him on their return". The gods have visited men — Im-Hotep waits their return.

Von Daniken mentions various other Egyptian deities, and states:

> The Egyptian pantheon is just as confusing. The ancient texts of the people on the Nile also tell of mighty beings who traversed the firmament in boats. (p. 84)

He goes on to refer to a well-known text dedicated to the sun-god Ra which tells of him drawing the ship of Aten (the sun disk) across the heavens. He quotes another inscription from one of the Pyramids which states that it is Ra who "directs the sun ship of millions of years" (p. 84). These are supposedly chariots of the gods.

The god Ptah is singled out for special attention — he being the god Ra when he is especially associated with the ancient Phaaronic city of Memphis. Again we quote:

> Need I add that when the god Ptah came to give the king the models (celebrating the anniversaries of his reign — Ed.) he appeared in a gleaming heavenly chariot and afterwards disappeared over the horizon in it. Today representations of the winged sun and a soaring falcon carrying the sign of eternity and eternal life can still be found on doors and temples at Edfu. (p. 84)

We also learn in the same explanation that the celebration was to take place for "six times a hundred thousand years".

THE CREATION OF EGYPTIAN GODS

According to the text known as "The Memphite Theology" Ptah created the other gods by thinking them into being. Another Egyptian text has the creator sun-god originally coming from the waters of chaos — a development associated with the functioning of eight strange gods such as Darkness and Primeval Ocean. How they can be earlier than the creator-god is not explained.

Other legends have the king participating in the journeys of the sun. I. E. S. Edwards writes:

> Every day the king would accompany the sun-god on his voyage across the skies. Sometimes he is described as a rower in the barque, . . . Elsewhere he is promoted to the position of captain of the barque. (p. 33)

This sort of legend and religious folk-lore is just as capable of belief as the literal acceptance of von Daniken's "gleaming heavenly chariot" for Ptah, to which we have referred. The whole idea of the gods being associated with a heavenly ship is simply a natural explanation of the recurring cycle of day and night — as darkness comes, the gods of the day are conquered by those of the night, but the day gods will know a resurrection the next morning. Similar legends are associated with the gods of the Canaanites — and other peoples.

It is surprising to read of such "chariots" as boosters for the argument that the gods visited mankind, utilizing vehicles such as these. It surely takes much less "faith" to accept the Christian concept of almighty God Who controlled the universe, Who spoke and it was done, the God Who revealed Himself in the Person of His Son Jesus Christ.

CHAPTER 9

MYTHOLOGIES, LEGENDS AND THE TRUE GOD

Von Daniken refers to a number of other gods as he brings together old mythologies to show that various peoples believed in visits from the gods. The author of "Chariots" touches on too many religions in passing to be able to deal with them all thoroughly in a work of limited size, but basically the traditions of peoples around the world are similar to those we have already mentioned. For example when Austen Layard excavated the Biblical Nineveh he found various images of their gods. In one of his books he describes some of these, and then says:

> Before the altar, on which were some sacrificial utensils, was the sacred chariot, with its elaborate yoke.

So the Assyrian gods had chariots. But the chariot was also the property of the Assyrian King Sennacherib — known in the Bible at such places as Isaiah chapter 37. This, then, was a "chariot of the gods" in an Assyrian palace. But unfortunately for von Daniken's hypotheses it was just an ordinary chariot, with very earth-bound horses depicted as the "motor-power".

THE MAYAS OF CENTRAL AMERICA

Another group to whom he refers is that people known as the Mayas of Central America. He hypothesises that they made calculations by means of an electronic brain (p. 76). This certainly is not the generally-held view of archaeologists — but we have already seen that that does not especially concern von Daniken, who set himself up as an authority beyond the accepted scholarship of that realm. But let it at least be stated that archaeologists do not credit these early Central Americans with established writing until about the 5th century A.D., and even if writing were known when their civilization is believed to have commenced about a thousand years earlier, there is clearly no thought of such a people having knowledge of astronomical details that could be accurately dated back to 27,000 years ago.

THAT "MIRACLE" JADE FROM CHINA

One continues to read on about these fantastic Latin American sites, all the more amazing because of the seeming new knowledge available to von Daniken. Thus at pages 116-117 we learn another fact about this Mayan civilization—

> The fantastic five-strand necklace of green jade in the burial pyramid of Tikal in Guatemala is a miracle. A miracle because the jade comes from China.

Actually it should not be a miracle even by von Daniken's own arguments, for if the Babylonian "Epic of Gilgamesh" could originate from South America as he suggests (p. 69), why could not jade have been imported from China — where is the miracle?

But in fact jade is readily plentiful in the river beds and mountains of Latin America. Here are two brief selections from Thomas Gann's "Maya Cities":

> Around this skeleton (of a young child—Ed.) were scattered broadcast a large handful of pieces of jade, some crude and unpolished, others partly worked, and others apparently fragments of broken ornaments. (p. 195)

With the skull (of a young adult—Ed.) in the northernmost temple was found a small necklace of very fine jade beads. (p. 198)

We read of jade being used as ear plugs (p. 242) and even to plug holes in teeth! (p. 243)

One need only consult the references to "jade" in J. Eric S. Thompson's "Rise and Fall of Maya Civilization" to realize that this was relatively plentiful. This quotation is from that source:

> Equally valuable was jade. One ancient work site of the mineral has been found in the Sierra de Las Minas in the north-eastern highlands, and no doubt others will be located. Jade was a symbol of wealth but also had religious associations. For instance, a jade bead was frequently placed in the mouth of a dead person of rank. Jades were offered in sacrifice and used in divination. (pp 20-21)

One chief was found with a magnificent mask consisting of two hundred pieces of jade arranged over his face, while a jade ring was on each finger. There were also necklaces and wrist pieces, the total count of jade pieces in that one tomb being 978! (p. 79)

But of course J. Eric S. Thompson writes as an archaeologist, and we have already seen von Daniken's opinion of archaeologists. How many "Chinese miracles" must there have been amongst those ancient Mayas!

PYRAMIDS AS BURIAL SITES

But in any case, von Daniken leaves us confused in this section. Elsewhere he ridicules the possibility of a pyramid being "nothing more than the burial place of an extravagant king! Anyone who can believe that explanation is welcome to it. . . ." (pp. 102-3) But now we learn of other huge pyramids which ARE the burial places of men after all. Or are they assembly places for the gods? (p. 120) Who IS confused?

We saw that von Daniken has these early American people as the first to have the Epic of Gilgamesh with its Flood story (p. 69). He sees similarities between "the religious legends of the pre-Inca peoples" and the records of the Sumerians, Assyrians, Babylonians and Egyptians (p. 76). We do not argue with that — in fact, we agree that there are very great similarities, for we accept the argument that there is a Satanic delusion — an attempt to blind the eyes of men by allowing them to have near-truth, sufficiently "acceptable" when it seems there must be some explanation beyond the confines of human activity.

However, we most certainly DO NOT agree with von Daniken's linking all these latter together as "cuneiform". Egyptian hieroglyphics and Babylonian cuneiform were basically different forms of writing — cuneiform was angular writing, dug into clay with a stylus-type of pen, whereas hieroglyphics was a cursive script, often using vegetable dyes, or charcoal, and written across the face of papyrus.

THE FEATHERED SERPENT

Von Daniken correctly associates the feathered serpent with the Mayas, and it is not difficult to see a connection with the serpent worshipped in Egypt and Canaan, and the serpent-like sirrush that appears so prolifically on the Ishtar Gate and Procession Way of ancient Babylon. There are interesting theories about the Mayas and Aztecs bringing primitive religious ideas with them from South-east Asia, but no one really knows. The similarity can as well be explained by the universal sameness of the nature of man, and by the existence of false gods willing to give some knowledge of spiritual realities so long as the real truth was kept hidden.

But visits of gods in space chariots? That IS a good imagination — credulity gone wild. What if we were to tell of that African legend of a woman who was pounding away at yams, when suddenly she raised her pole too high and it hit the sky-god 'Nyame in the face. Who would believe it? But it is in fact a primitive African legend.

"DRAUNIKOU" IN FIJI

And there are many more like it. Well do I remember one night in Fiji, sitting entranced as I listened to some of the legends and folk-lore of the Islands. I heard all about "draunikou" — a priest buries a piece of a man's hair, and soon that man dies: rather like "pointing the bone" with the Australian aborigines. One specially interesting story was about a man who forgot to throw a bowl of kava (the native drink) over the side of his fishing boat as an offering to the shark god. A little while later his child was born, and it had the face of a shark.

Interesting. Fascinating. Sometimes frightening. But to be taken seriously as literal fact? Draunikou can be of course, for there are psychological possibilities there, but other legends are clearly not acceptable to reasoning people. After all, the shark-faced baby is never shown. And the legends of such people are not put down in writing until they themselves become "educated".

THE DISAPPEARANCE OF THE MAYAN CIVILIZATION

But let us return to that mystery of the Mayan civilization which disappeared — according to the author of "Chariots" — about 600 A.D. (p. 121). I found myself bargaining for artefacts from the Mayan civilization on a recent trip to Latin America, and at the time undertook a little further research. Historians date the passing of this civilization at over 200 years later than the time given by von Daniken.

The interesting conjecture then follows in "Chariots" that because the Mayan civilization disappeared without trace, the people must have trekked far to the north where they established another kingdom, with temples and pyramids erected according to the precise instructions of the gods — gods who had let the people down by not returning to the previous centre, as expected! Von Daniken says concerning his way-out explanation of the disappearance of this civilization:

> I should like to introduce a new note into the concert of opinions, a theory that is not proved any more than the other interpretations are. But regardless of the probability of the other explanations, I venture to make my contribution boldly and with conviction. (p. 122)

We do not object to the author making his unconfirmed speculation "boldly and with conviction" if it were not that he then presents his theories as though they were fact. Thus he presents a stone relief found in the region as a god, and says—

> Our space traveller — he is clearly depicted as one. . . . The astronaut's front seat is separated by struts from the rear portion of the vehicle . . . (p. 124).

He states a hypothesis, then accepts it as fact. In philosophical terms, von Daniken is guilty of many *non-sequiters* — he makes jumps in his argument that are not justified by the evidence he presents. He jumps to conclusions which demand the acceptability of his earlier hypotheses — at times with little "proof" as to the valid connection between argument and conclusion.

Erich von Daniken states that various theories have been put forward to explain the sudden abandonment of this ancient centre of culture, none of them convincing. But this can be said about other sites as well — trade routes change, earthquakes destroy thousands of people while thousands of others leave through fear, wars cause deportations of tens of thousands (witness the history of Israel and Judah); and even climatic changes can be pointed to as the cause of major shifts of population.

We do not always know the answer — as with the legendary Atlantis. But now it seems that Atlantis was more than just legend, and there is serious thought that the city lies buried beneath the sea. And what about the mystery of that high place at Bab-edh Dra'a on the Moabite foothills? Apparently nobody visited it for something like 600 years, and it is at least possible that this was because the inhabitants of Sodom and Gomorrah and the other cities had been buried under the Dead Sea. In general terms, this could fit the dates of the Biblical incident.

Here, then, are two cases where there has been mystery as to the whereabouts of previous inhabitants. Neither is resolved by a space-gods theory, and von Daniken has not made out a convincing case for the Mayan civilization to have disappeared because of the activity of space-gods either. It is not an "either-or" case with space men the alternative — even if it does make an interesting story.

BUT DID THE CIVILIZATION DISAPPEAR ENTIRELY?

Erich von Daniken makes much of this supposed sudden disappearance of the Mayan civilization — so complete was this "absolutely incredible thing" that "no inhabitant ever returned there" (p. 121).

However, this is at least partially opposed to the facts. First, it is very debatable that the civilization did disappear entirely. J. Eric S. Thompson is recognized as a leading authority in the field, and he suggests that a series of "peasants' revolts" occurred in which the rulers were killed, but that the peoples returned for religious purposes from time to time, even after the buildings had collapsed. He presents conclusive evidence, such as bodies above the debris of collapsed rooms, as well as every-day utensils such as pottery and spindle-whorls — all clearly ABOVE the debris of the collapsed room (pp. 106-7).

Thompson suggests that "it is incorrect to suppose that this vast area had been a vacuum for hundreds of years" (p. 104). He proves his point by specific details of particular areas where settlements were known to have continued over the centuries. He tells of periodic visits to the actual religious sites themselves, and even of half-hearted attempts by the masons to keep the sites "in service" (p. 106).

All this clearly opposes von Daniken's sweeping assertion that "no inhabitant ever returned there". Interestingly enough, Thompson's views are a challenge to earlier strongly-held archaeological opinion at various points. They indicate that archaeologists are men of science, ready to face new alternatives as the case demands. This is radically different from the supposed dogmatism of archaeologists to which we have already referred by quoting von Daniken (p. 7).

. . . . . .

In this chapter we have seen something of the legends of the Mayas and of other ancient peoples. We shall comment on one more of these ancient records to which von Daniken has referred — this time we consider an Assyrian legend.

FLYING CHARIOTS OF ASSYRIA

Very many of the ancient legends about gods and flying chariots and magical powers are in the same category. Von Daniken himself has taken one of these legends to show that "God" is an astronaut, but this "astronaut" is in fact Ashur, one of the leading Assyrian gods.

In his notation concerning this picture von Daniken hypothesises that "The object in the centre is described as a sacred tree. It could just as reasonably be interpreted as a symbolic representation of the construction of an atom, with an astronaut in a fiery chariot above."

To say the least, Erich von Daniken has a good imagination. He has these ancient people knowing all about the construction of the complex atom — though in fact the object shown is widely known as, and IS, a tree.

As we have said, his astronaut is no less than the Assyrian god Ashur. He is holding a bow and arrow, which is rather surprising for an "astronaut".

However, as von Daniken says,

> NOTHING is incredible any longer . . . So let us stick tenaciously to our theory, according to which astronauts from distant planets visited the earth thousands of years ago. We know that our ingenuous and primitive forefathers did not know what to make of the astronauts' superior technology. They worshipped the astronauts as "gods" who came from other stars . . . (p. 47)

TOO MANY MISINTERPRETATIONS!

This is typical of the approach of "Chariots". His theory depends on such misinterpretations as that concerning Ashur, and on the total acceptance of traditions that have grown in the telling around the camp fires of the centuries. But we are to "stick tenaciously to our theory". And that is not all — for "we know. . . ." So it is no longer a theory. It has become fact.

Is this the basis on which thousands of people the world over are to follow this totally unacceptable teaching whereby the Christian's almighty God is reduced to the status of some visitor from the regions of the sky thousands of years ago?

Surely the chariots of von Daniken's wild imagination must soon go crashing into the oblivion of forgetfulness.

THE GOD OF "CHARIOTS" AND THE GOD OF THE BIBLE

Belief in that God does not lead to the humanism put forward by Erich von Daniken, nor to a belief in a golden age ushered in by the realization of the benefits of the space age. Nor does it lead to the belief that mankind's main objective is to "colonise the universe" nor that his "whole spiritual duty" is to "perpetuate his efforts and practical experience" (p. 119). "Then," according to von Daniken, will be fulfilled "the promise of the 'gods' of peace on earth" with its further assurance that "the way to heaven open can come true".

This humanistic approach is very different from the spiritual realities which underlie the challenge of God to man. Each man has a responsibility to his fellows, but this does not centre around new civilizations and new space colonies. It relates to this special planet Earth, created by God and given to man as his home.

But man is also a spiritual being, with needs extending beyond the physical and the material. God has provided for those spiritual needs to be met, and so made it possible for man to live in fellowship with Himself. That is the whole purpose of the Christian Gospel — that God is made known in the Person of Jesus Christ Who died on a cross to give man forgiveness of sins and new life with God.

This is not the god whom von Daniken presents, nor is his concept of "god" acceptable to Christian people; in fact his presentation is objectionable.

Let us glance at several examples. He tells of the arrival of the god Kukulkan amongst the Mayan people, an old man with a beard and a white robe. This "god" taught all the people "all the sciences, arts and customs and left very wise laws. It was said that under his direction corn-cobs grew as big as a man and that cotton grew already coloured" (p. 127).

Leaving aside the argument that the Mayan legend is associated with the Toltecs in the 10th century A.D., it is clear that this is NOT the Jesus of the Gospels. Von Daniken himself admits this, for this "visitor" clearly did not teach the Mayas the use of the wheel and the cart, which were never used by the Mayas (p. 128). Then why mention it? Why tell us that "A kind of Messianic role is attributed to him . . ."? (p. 128)

Why are we later told concerning unidentified flying objects (at page 147) that "Among the religious fanatics, the Egyptian 'UFO angel' naturally comes from Mohammed, the Asiatic one from Buddha and the Christian one directly from Jesus"?

Turning to page 71 what is meant by his emphasis on the "intellectual" when he states that "with the space age, the *intellectual* Day of Judgment comes ever nearer. The theological clouds will evaporate, scattered like shreds of mist"? Is the "only one god" whom he suggests the Christian God of the Bible? What does he imply by "Without being unbelieving, we can no longer afford to be credulous"? These questions indicate that "Chariots of the Gods?" presents forthright opposition to the beliefs of Christian people concerning God and theology.

Von Daniken tells us quite clearly "I claim that we cannot possess the 'truth' . . . Anyone who really seeks THE truth cannot and ought not to seek it under the aegis and within the confines of his own religion" (p. 73). The Bible teaching is that Jesus Christ is Himself the Truth, the only way to the Father (John 14:6).

ARCHAEOLOGY AND THE BIBLE

Von Daniken appears to have a special "thing" against archaeology, as we have already pointed out. In fact, it was because of this that a number of people urged me to write this survey. He refers to the evidence from archaeology verifying facts in the Old Testament, then states that such verified facts are not proof as to the religion itself. He argues that such finds merely show that people lived in a particular area, but "they do not prove that the God of that people was the one and only god (and not a space traveller)" (p. 73).

In another of my booklets, "Archaeology and the Bible Student", four specific points are made as to the relevance of archaeology for the Bible student. These are summarised on the first two pages of that booklet as follows:

(a) Archaeology has confirmed the accuracy of many Bible incidents and stories;

(b) Archaeology shows that many customs of ancient peoples are recorded in the Scriptures;

(c) Archaeology has added to our knowledge of peoples and lands of the Bible; and

(d) Archaeology has endorsed the meaning of many words and phrases which previously were unknown.

Numerous examples are given, and this adds up to a convincing presentation of the claim that the Bible is the world's most remarkably accurate history textbook. But it also demonstrates that the Old Testament writings were written against the backgrounds claimed for them. We have already referred to Messianic prophecies, those remarkable Old Testament pre-writings which the Christian sees fulfilled in Jesus Christ. Their genuineness is attested in various ways, not the least being that the men who wrote such accurate history — as archaeological research demonstrates — also wrote those prophecies.

We do not need to argue that "archaeology proves the Bible". The Bible seems quite able to vindicate itself. Someone has said that it is like a lion: let it loose and it looks after itself. But this is the Book that gives us the knowledge of God in Jesus Christ, and it is well said that the closer one draws to this Book, the closer one draws to God, and to his fellow-man.

According to the Bible (e.g. at John 14:6, Acts 4:12), it is not true that all religions are one, or that it matters little by what name we worship God. The Bible makes it clear that God is a jealous God, not to be equated with Baal or any other false god of the surrounding nations.

We have demonstrated that there are opposing evil powers, and von Daniken himself recognizes the widespread nature of this belief. He links the serpent with evil as he states:

> "Primaeval image of evil, the snake is condemned to crawl. How could anyone worship this repulsive creature as a god and why could it fly into the bargain? Among the Mayas it could." (p. 127)

It is indeed a strange thing, yet here again the original source can be traced to the record at Genesis chapter 3. It is interesting to compare those early chapters of Genesis with the Sumerian "Epic of Emmerkar" which tells of the "pure" land of Bilmun where "the lion killed not, the wolf snatched not the lamb" (S. H. Hooke, "Middle Eastern Mythology," p. 114). Once again, we can see the uncorrupted original in the Bible record of the Garden of Eden.

Our point is that even the author of "Chariots" acknowledges the presence of evil spiritual powers. The Bible clearly teaches that their leader is Satan, and that at times he masquerades as an angel of light. He is quite willing for individual men and women to have some INTELLECTUAL perception of God, so long as they do not come to SPIRITUAL perception as well, and grasp the true reality.

Thus, as we study various ideas about the gods prevalent among the nations, we see an occasional gleam of light.

"ALL THE FULLNESS OF THE GODHEAD BODILY"

Many of their ideas about God or gods we utterly reject, but it is yet true that the better ideas can be seen to perfection in the Person of Jesus Christ. Concepts of truth, justice, righteousness, light — and others — are linked with various gods. The ultimate of these is seen in the Person and teachings of Jesus Christ. He is no "heavenly charioteer", but the Son of God in Whom dwells "all the fullness of the Godhead bodily" (Colossians 2:9).

On this note we conclude. The answer to Erich von Daniken's question on the cover of his book, "Was God an astronaut?" is easily answered. No. The true God, the Almighty, is the One Whose character is consistently presented in the pages of both Old and New Testaments.

AN APPENDIX TO "CRASH GO THE CHARIOTS!"

By Clifford Wilson, Ph.D.

CLIFFORD WILSON TALKS TO A PHYSICIST ABOUT "CHARIOTS"

A Dialogue with Dr. Frederick H. Giles, Jnr., Associate Professor, Department of Physics and Astronomy, University of South Carolina, Columbia, S.C., U.S.A.

WILSON: In his book "Chariots of the Gods?" Erich von Daniken writes at length about other planetary systems. Can you explain why it is conjectured that there are other systems besides that which includes the earth?

GILES: One point often advanced is that our sun is itself a star similar to many others, so why would there not be other planetary systems?

HOW WOULD PLANETS ORIGINATE?

WILSON: If there were such systems, how would their origin be explained?

GILES: If planets came into being during the life history of particular stars, there is a feasible explanation. Some of the younger stars seem to be rotating relatively rapidly as compared with stars which are a little older, and there appears to be rather an abrupt change in the rotating characteristics of these older stars as compared with the younger — a change that apparently takes place at a particular age point.

WILSON: So what is the conjecture — how is this changed rotating characteristic related to the formation of planets?

GILES: One possibility is that as stars grow older and pass through this particular age point, they tend to throw off planets, and that the extra spin of the younger stars is then taken up by the new planet or planets which are moving around the star. Thus, according to this theory, the star itself would rotate less rapidly.

WILSON: So this theory would explain why the star at a certain age appears to rotate less rapidly, but are any of these supposed new planets visible?

GILES: It would be virtually impossible to see such planets as we see stars. They are essentially invisible — they do not emit light of themselves, and they would be very small relative to the size of the star around which they would revolve.

WILSON: So these "planets" would not be other stars but smaller throw-offs?

GILES: They would be more in the nature of a satellite — not other stars or planets really; another name is "dark companion" or "dark binary". Such a "dark companion" could even be a great piece of rock.

WHAT EVIDENCE OF OTHER PLANETS?

WILSON: You have said it would be impossible to see such a "dark companion", but I gather its presence could be indicated by the changed rotating characteristic of a star — would you elaborate?

GILES: The theory is that if there was such a dark companion its presence would be indicated by an irregular wobble in the star itself as the planet revolved around it, much as there is a wobble of the earth as the moon goes around it every 30 days.

WILSON: Is there any direct evidence that there ARE other planetary systems?

GILES: No. There is one other case where the inference from the "wobble" points to another planet — this exception is known as "Barnard's Star".

This star has a measurable wobble — the wobble is very slight, but it is measurable. This could indicate that there is a dark companion to this star — a satellite.

WILSON: Would the distances involved make the detection of such wobbles difficult?

GILES: Yes. Even the nearest star is four light years away, and the detection of a wobble is very difficult. Light travels at 186,000 miles per second — and when we realize that the nearest star is four light years away it becomes clear that theories about other planets are highly conjectural.

WILSON: You have already said that it is only conjecture that there are other planetary systems. What about life on von Daniken's conjectured planets — is that possible?

GILES: Von Daniken begins with the arguments of Harlow Shapley who was a Harvard astronomer. Shapley was one of those early astronomers of modern times who became convinced that man is too apt to see himself as the center of all things, and he writes belittling man's place. He stresses that our system is not even at the center of the galaxy. Shapley's conjectures are by no means universally accepted by astro-physicists, and in fact they have been widely challenged. But his arguments are in a very different category from von Daniken's in "Chariots of the Gods?", as with this statement from "Chariots"—

> There is no doubt about the existence of planets similar to the earth — with a similar mixture of atmospheric gases, similar gravity, similar flora and possibly even similar fauna. (p. 17)

All this is based on Shapley's writings, but it jumps rapidly from a legitimate (though controversial) conjecture to "There is no doubt".

WILSON: At page 165 of "Chariots" the author refers to a "secret conference" that took place in November, 1961, in the National Radio Astronomy Observatory at Green Bank in West Virginia. You have shown me a copy of a report of this conference. Would you care to comment?

GILES: It was not a "secret conference" and the report is openly published.

WILSON: I see it emanates from the Goddard Space-Flight Center, NASA. Do its propositions agree with those of von Daniken?

GILES: Not at all. Let me give you a typical quote from just one page:

> Estimation of the fraction of stars which form planets is subject to great uncertainty and, although several different arguments may be adduced, they are all weak. . . . Estimation of the average number of planets per system with environments suitable for the development of life, is a matter of pure guesswork. Mass, composition, temperature, and many other factors are important. Little as we know of the probability of occurrence of planetary systems, we know nothing of the details of any other planetary system but our own. (J. P. T. Pearman, p. 289 in "Extraterrestrial Intelligent Life and Interstellar Communication: An Informal Discussion".)

This conference discussed the probability or otherwise of intelligent life on other planets, but the point should be made very strongly that the whole approach was diametrically opposed to von Daniken's statement that "There is no doubt" as to the existence of other planets. This conference openly stated that such a conjecture was a matter of "pure guesswork".

WILSON: Could you outline briefly what you see as the problems associated with intelligent life on other planets?

GILES: We have already seen that the first problem is, "Are there other planets anyway?" Then if there is even one such planet, will it have the right conditions for the maintaining of life — such conditions as the right temperature range. For example, if the temperature is too high the complexity of the chemical processes is such that they simply do not hold together. If the temperature is too low, the chemical processes do not occur rapidly enough for living things to arrive at a point of change, and therefore even the process of thinking would be out of the question. So it follows that if we are thinking of a form of life that involves chemistry, the temperature range is very important. And there are other problems: such a planet must be commodious — it must not be too heavy or it would plaster life to its earth; it must not be too light, for some sort of atmosphere would need to be maintained. Then too the conjectured planet must be the right distance from the star it spun off, and also there needs to be a fantastically long period of time for the emergence of a self-replicating system. Even if we accepted the theory that life on this planet is between 2 and 5 billion years old, that still would not give any assurance of the development of life anywhere else. And we might well ask ourselves, "How much time have we got to allow for such development?"

WILSON: You talk about "life" — do you mean intelligent life that existed billions of years ago?

GILES: No—just "life". The emergence of sentient, conscious, intelligent life involves further problems. If all the other conditions were met — all the problems we have already discussed — we would still need enough time for the complexity of intelligent life to appear. And even if there were intelligent beings, that does not necessarily mean that their technology would be highly developed. It would be an exceedingly complex operation for them to communicate with beings on earth or any other planet — even if they had the tremendous periods of time necessary for such an operation. Even at a conservative estimate it would take four light years for such a signal to be sent and received on earth, and then four more light years for the return signal. By that time the original operators would have been long since dead.

VON DANIKEN'S INSUPPORTABLE THEORIES

WILSON: Am I right in concluding that von Daniken's hypotheses are not supported by facts?

GILES: Yes — the points I have made are only some of the ways in which von Daniken's hypothesis is quite unacceptable. His arguments are interesting but not really supportable. If we apply our minds to it, we can come up with any kind of theory we want to, but the question is, Is it supported by facts, or is it just science fiction? I recently came across an article by Martin Gardner in "The Scientific American" which bears on this point. Gardner points out that since the beginning of history "unusual coincidences have strengthened belief in the influence on life of occult forces." Relating this to von Daniken's book, in this case it appears that "unusual coincidences have strengthened belief in the influence on life" of non-terrestrial intelligent beings. It is possible to take disconnected facts from the mass of material available and make a seemingly connected presentation, and this is what von Daniken has done. He has picked up some of the most conjectural areas of physics and astronomy and selected his own array of quite unconnected facts or suppositions, then built on them as though they were established and connected facts. In that article I referred to, Martin Gardner quotes G. K. Chesterton, "Life is full of a ceaseless shower of small coincidences . . . It is this that lends a frightful plausibility to all false doctrines and evil fads. There are always such props of accidental arguments upon anything."

WILSON: Would you state once more the basis for the conjecture that there are other planets?

GILES: The only planet that we know for sure has life on it is the earth. One other star has been detected with a slight wobble, and this could mean that it has an invisible dark companion moving around it. Such a dark companion would make the star itself wobble. As a very slight wobble has been measured in relation to one star, some astronomers conjecture that the wobble is caused by a planet rotating around the planet.

VON DANIKEN'S LACK OF SCIENTIFIC PRECISION

WILSON: That seems rather flimsy evidence for von Daniken's statement that undoubtedly there are other planets similar to the earth!

GILES: What you say is right. Even if astronomers calculate in terms of probability for such bodies — and some do — they never use the terms of certainty which von Daniken does. His hypotheses simply do not fit the facts. But that is typical of his approach at many places. He has not the precision expected of scientific writing.

WILSON: Could you give another example?

GILES: Well, at page 158 he writes about the *exact* measurement of *about* 10 milliard light years! Then at page 159 he seems to be suggesting that laser light beams travel faster than radio — his wording is somewhat ambiguous, but the fact is that laser light travels no faster than radio waves.

Von Daniken's whole approach is open to question, and his interpretations are often distorted. One example is where he suggests that physicists at Princeton made a certain discovery relating to elementary particles, and that this new discovery was theoretically impossible. The physicists would deny that emphatically. They would agree that what they observed did not fit into the currently accepted theory, but this may be the fault of the initial interpretation, or the theory might not have been sufficiently comprehensive to handle the new situation. If so, the theory would need to be changed or modified or expanded to accommodate the new facts, and the physicists would be the first to admit it. In this particular case there have been a number of experiments carried out to see just what revision should be made to the theory. There have been checks on whether the experiment was poorly done, or whether there was an initial error, or possibly even to find out if the theory is inadequate. If this last is true, there are exciting new possibilities.

A FINAL COMMENT

WILSON: What is your final comment about von Daniken's book, "Chariots of the Gods?"

GILES: He takes conjectures, accepts them as fact, builds on to them way-out theories, and presents his "many small coincidences" according to his own preconceived notions. He deliberately chooses the unconnected, weaves a semblance of connection around it, and puts his theories out as foregone conclusions. This approach is often used by writers, and it may make exciting reading, but one dare not accept it as substantially credible.

BIBLIOGRAPHY

ALBRIGHT, W. F. *Recent Discoveries in Bible Lands.* Funk & Wagnalls Co., New York, 1936.

ALBRIGHT, W. F. *Yahweh and the Gods of Canaan. An Historical Analysis of Two Contrasting Faiths.* Athlone Press, University of London, 1968.

ALBRIGHT, W. F. *Archaeological Discovery and the Scriptures* — Christianity Today, vol. XII, Number 19, June 1968

ALBRIGHT, William Foxwell, *From the Stone Age to Christianity.* First published in 1940 by The Johns Hopkins Press, Baltimore. Re-issued revised by Doubleday Anchor Books 1946 and 1957.

ALBRIGHT, William Foxwell, *The Biblical Period from Abraham to Ezra.* Harper & Row, New York, Revised and Expanded Edition, 1963.

BARNETT, R. D. *Illustrations of Old Testament History* British Museum Publication, 1968.

BEASLEY, W. J. *The Amazing Story of Sodom.* Gospel Literature Service, Bombay, 1957.

BOYD, R. T. *Tells, Tombs and Treasures. A Pictorial Guide to Biblical Archaeology.* Baker Book House, Grand Rapids, Michigan, 1950.

BOUQUET, A. C. *Sacred Books of the World.* Penguin, London, 1954.

BURIED HISTORY — Quarterly Journal of the Australian Institute of Archaeology, Melbourne.

CAMERON, A. G. W. (Ed.), Report on *Extraterrestrial Intelligent Life and Interstellar Communications: An Informal Discussion."* Institute for Space Studies, Goddard Space-Flight Center, NASA, published by W. A. Benjamin Inc.,

CERAM, C. W., *A Picture History of Archaeology,* Thames and Hudson, London, 1963.

CHILDE, Gordon. *What Happened in History.* Pelican, London.

CIVILIZATION PAST AND PRESENT, volume 1, published by Scott, Foresman & Company, 1960.

De CAMP, L. S. and de CAMP, C. C., *Citadels of Mystery,* Fontana-Collins, London, 1972.

De PAOR, Liam. *Archaeology — an Illustrated Introduction.* Penguin.

EDWARDS, I. E. S., *The Pyramids of Egypt,* Penguin, Victoria, Australia, 1970.

FAKHRY, Ahmed, *The Pyramids,* University of Chicago Press, Chicago, 1969.

FINEGAN, Jack, *Light from the Ancient Past.* Princeton University Press, New Jersey, 1959.

FREE, Joseph P. *Archaeology and Bible History,* 2nd ed. Wheaton, Ill. Scripture Press. 1950.

GANN, Thomas, *Maya Cities,* Duckworth, London, 1927.

GARNER, Gordon. *Chariots of the Gods — a Critical Review.* Aust. Institute of Archaeology, Melbourne, 1972.

GLUECK, Nelson. *Rivers in the Desert*. Philadelphia: Jewish Publication Society, 1959.
GOETZ, Delia and MORLEY, Sylvanus G., *Popol Vuh*. From the Spanish Translation by Adrian Recinos; University of Oklahoma Press, Norman, U.S.A., 1950.
HEYERDAHL, Thor, *Aku-Aku — The Secret of Easter Island*, George Allen and Unwin Ltd., London, 1958.
HEYERDAHL, Thor, *The Kon-Tiki Expedition*, George Allen and Unwin Ltd., London, 1950.
LEWIS, H. D., and SLATER, R. L. *The Study of Religions* Pelican, 1966.
PARROT, Andre. *The Tower of Babel*. New York Philosophical Library.
PFEIFFER, Charles F. *The Patriarchal Age*. Grand Rapids: Baker Book House, 1961.
PRITCHARD, James B. (ed.), ***Ancient Near East in Pictures Relating to the Old Testament***. Princeton: Princeton University Press, 1950.
PRITCHARD, J. B., *Ancient Near Eastern Texts Relating to the Old Testament*, Princeton University Press, New Jersey, 1955.
PLAGUES OF EGYPT, Reprint from *Buried History*. Melb
SHAPLEY, Harlow, *Of Stars and Men*, Beacon Press, Boston, New York and Amsterdam, 1963.
1958.
THOMPSON, John Arthur. *The Bible and Archaeology*. Grand Rapids: Wm. B. Eerdmans Publishing Co., 1962.
THOMPSON, J. Eric S., *The Rise and Fall of Maya Civilization*, University of Oklahoma Press, Norman, U.S.A., 1966.
UNGER, Merrill F. *Archaeology and the Old Testament*. Grand Rapids: Zondervan Publishing House, 1954.
UNGER'S BIBLE DICTIONARY, Moody Press, Chicago.
Von DANIKEN, Erich, *Chariots of the Gods?* Corgi Books, London, 1972.
VOS, Howard V. *Genesis and Archaeology*. Moody Press.
WILSON, Clifford. *In the Beginning God . . .* Word of Truth Productions, Melbourne, 1970.
WILSON, Clifford. *Exploring the Old Testament*. Word of Truth Productions, Melbourne, 1970.
WILSON, Clifford. *Old Testament Backgrounds*. Word of Truth Productions, Melbourne, 1970.
WILSON, Clifford. *Archaeology and the Bible Student*. Aust. Institute of Archaeology, Melbourne, 1968.
WISEMAN, D. J. *Illustrations from Biblical Archaeology*. Grand Rapids: Wm. B. Eerdmans Publishing Co. 1958.
WISEMAN, P. J. *New Discoveries in Babylonia About Genesis*. Marshall, Morgan and Scott, London, 1946.
Wycliffe Bible Commentary, The Southwestern Company, Nashville, Tennessee, 1962.

ACKNOWLEDGMENTS:

My academic interest in archaeology goes back 25 years to undergraduate days, and it was my privilege to commence lecturing in the subject when I joined the Australian Institute of Archaeology in 1954. Acknowledgment is due to the President and others associated with that Institute for the measure of expertize gained through that association.

In between my early association with that Institute and my later return as Director, I spent a number of years as Senior Lecturer with the Melbourne Bible Institute, with special involvement in teaching of the Old Testament. In a sense this too was training for the writing of a book such as this, and a debt of gratitude is due to the late Rev. John Searle, former Principal. The encouragement he gave in many ways was really valuable in the utilization of my archaeological knowledge.

In the specific task of writing this "alternative" to Erich von Daniken's presentation, special thanks is due to my wife, Avis, for her continued co-operation and encouragement, and to my son, Rev. David Wilson, who so capably helped at various points of research. Geoffrey Beel is another who helped in this way.

Mr and Mrs Frank Schenk are personal friends who were responsible for the setting and correction of the proofs. They worked into the nights to have this completed before my own return to a University position at the University of South Carolina in the United States.

To each of these my very real thanks is offered.

INDEX OF MAJOR TOPICS

A Novel Of Terror—In The Tradition Of
THE EXORCIST and THE OTHER

THE DIABOLIST

by

Paul W. Fairman

(#75-411 95¢)

First it was Uncle Amby's voice on the telephone, a desperate voice pleading, "Help me! Help me!" And Hal Brent knew he had to do whatever he could to help him . . . even though Uncle Amby had been dead for two days.

Then it was the voice of the woman who called herself Margo Dillon, threatening Hal. His sister Lisa was in the hands of a strange Satan-worshipping cult, and there was no telling what they would do to her unless he surrendered Uncle Amby's mysterious diary. Hal would do anything to help Lisa . . . but the diary was his only weapon against the cult.

Then the voices started invading his dreams, along with visions of fantastic evil and depravity, and he knew he had to act. But how? How can one man fight the forces of Hell—and the Prince of Darkness himself?